FEARFUL

TO

FEARLESS

biblical truths
to inspire you to live a life
free of fear and to worship God

Fear Not • Don't Worry • Fear God

Jeff Kusner

Fearful To Fearless
Copyright © 2010, 2011 by Jeff Kusner

KOOZZZ PUBLISHING
Mount Vernon, Ohio 43050

The Scripture versions used in this book are listed on page 209-210, which hereby becomes a part of this copyright page. Italics and bold formatting have been added by the author for emphasis.

Cover photo: Koozzz Photographic - www.koozzz.com

ISBN-13: 978-0-615-40232-1
ISBN-10: 0-615-40232-1
Library of Congress Control Number: 2010913526

Dedication

To Jesus, the ultimate example of courage, obedience and fearlessness, thank you for paying the price for me.

To my wife Chris, generous and beautiful in so many ways, who has stood by and supported me these many years. Thank you for your love and dedication.

To Jason (and Ashley) and Scott, thank you for the opportunity to experience life from the perspective of a father, and for making it easy for me. You are loved more than you know.

For family and friends, your friendship is priceless!

Table of Contents

Preface

I've certainly made my share of excuses when it comes to stepping out, but each time I've chosen to step in faith I have been blessed and enriched. I know it pleases God to see people answer His call. He has a plan and wants to include both you and me to accomplish it!

This book you are reading is something that has been on my heart for more than 10 years, I've actually been waiting for someone else to write it. I kept looking for something that you could pick up when you needed to hear a short word from God in the area of fear and worry.

A few years ago I felt a calling that was far outside my comfort zone, it was a sense that it was time to leave my job. Now, that is not something you decide to do on a whim, especially in these uncertain economic times. My wife, Chris, and I began to pray, and if that's what God had in store for us it would be okay. To ease the transition we began to pray specifically for a severance package, and I expressed my interest in the idea. A few months passed before we got wind of planned cutbacks, and I found myself praising God for His faithfulness as I received word of my pending departure. I think I caught the boss off guard with my attitude. It was almost as though he was the one that needed consoling. When I shared with my co-workers that it was a gift from God and an answer to prayer they were floored!

Upon leaving my job I was compelled to bring together the scriptures for this book. To dig in and pray about what each one had to say. The book you're reading is the result, it represents about a year and a half of research. Through the process there is one point that was repeated over and over, it is that God is with us, Emmanuel. In fact that's what God said to Moses when he first objected at the burning bush;

> *Moses answered God, "But why me? What makes you think that I could ever go to Pharaoh and lead the children of Israel out of Egypt?" "I'll be with you," God said.*

> *Exodus 3:11-12a (MSG)*

The account of Jesus calming the storm in Mark 4 was one of the primary inspirations in writing this book. It's an impressive demonstration of Christ's power over nature and His ability to comfort us in the storm.

On that day, when evening had come, he said to them, "Let us go across to the other side." And leaving the crowd, they took him with them in the boat, just as he was. And other boats were with him. And a great windstorm arose, and the waves were breaking into the boat, so that the boat was already filling. But he was in the stern, asleep on the cushion. And they woke him and said to him, "Teacher, do you not care that we are perishing?" And he awoke and rebuked the wind and said to the sea, "Peace! Be still!" And the wind ceased, and there was a great calm. He said to them, "Why are you so afraid? Have you still no faith?" And they were filled with great fear and said to one another, "Who then is this, that even the wind and the sea obey him?"

Mark 4:35-41 (ESV)

The scripture illustrates His willingness to respond when we call to Him in prayer, even though from our point of view it may seem that He is asleep when we call to Him.

When the disciples cried out suggesting that He didn't care whether they perished or not, Christ showed His disappointment in their lack of faith. For Christ loves us all and wants for none to perish, but for all to have faith and go through the storm with Him. Each time we choose to trust Him in the storm the stronger our faith becomes.

But what we also see in this passage is the transformation from being afraid, to having the fear of God. The disciples just witnessed the power that He had over the sea and storm and realized the power that He had over them. They were now in awe, they marveled at what they just observed and were filled with the fear of God, a godly fear of the power and grace of Christ during the calm, a fear of the Lord and all His goodness, a reverent awe that was full of honor and glorifying to Christ.

The aim of *Fearful to Fearless* is to bring together those passages that demonstrate or direct us to not be afraid, to not worry or be anxious, to look to Christ for strength and comfort, and be transformed to have a worshipful fear and awe of God.

This collection of biblically themed references consists of almost 400 scripture passages, each accompanied by a short biblical truth to help provide clarity and encouragement.

Fear Not

For God hath not given us the spirit of fear; but of power, and of love, and of a sound mind.

2 Timothy 1:7 (KJV)

"The wise man in the storm prays God, not for safety from danger, but for deliverance from fear."

~ Ralph Waldo Emerson

Fear is what we experience in response to a threat of danger, whether real or perceived. It is often accompanied by different physical responses in us such as increased heart rate, blood pressure, muscle tension and rapid breathing to name a few. In fact God created us in such a way that some bodily functions such as our digestion and immune systems actually shut down in those circumstances in order to channel more of our physical energy into protecting ourselves.

These are all built-in responses that are designed to help prepare us to either run or fight in dangerous situations. It's an instinct that we all possess.

Then there is the kind of fear that is unfounded, the kind of fear that tears us apart inside as we constantly hash and rehash things that might have been, or things we have no control over. The things we worry about day in and day out, that cause us to continually beat ourselves up. It's the kind of fear that prevents us from growing and experiencing joy and satisfaction. The kind of fear that holds us back from stepping out of our comfort zone for Christ and from experiencing God on a more intimate level as we continually make excuses for the things He's called us to do, which is just what Satan wants.

Even Moses made excuses when God was speaking to him at the burning bush;

Moses objected, "They won't trust me. They won't listen to a word I say. They're going to say, 'God? Appear to him? Hardly!'"

Exodus 4:1 (MSG)

Of course God had an answer for him, He told Moses to pick up his stick! So then Moses had to do some quick thinking to come up with some more excuses;

Moses raised another objection to God: "Master, please, I don't talk well. I've never been good with words, neither before nor after you spoke to me. I stutter and stammer." He said, "Oh, Master, please! Send somebody else!"

Exodus 4:10, 13 (MSG)

In response God told Moses that He would be with him when he speaks, and would give Moses the words to say.

The Bible is very clear when it comes to fear and the influences of the devil, in chapter 6 of the book of Ephesians we are told that our walk with God is to include putting on the full armor of God to defend ourselves.

Put on the full armor of God so that you can fight against the devil's evil tricks.

Ephesians 6:11 (NCV)

We are to wear the belt of truth, the breastplate of righteousness and to put on the shoes to stand firm in our desire to share the gospel. To take up the shield of faith, the helmet of God's saving power and the sword of the word of God that comes from the Spirit.

Nowhere in this text does it suggest that we put on any sort of armor to protect our backside as we flee in retreat. Instead we are to have the love of God in our lives, which is the ultimate solution to fear.

There is no fear in love. But perfect love drives out fear…

1 John 4:18 (NIV)

Join me as we explore God's compassionate and comforting words on fear that encourage us to become more bold, courageous, trusting and faithful for Him each day.

After these things the word of the LORD came unto Abram in a vision, saying, **Fear not**, Abram: I am thy shield, and thy exceeding great reward.

Genesis 15:1 (KJV)

Do not be afraid or intimidated by the revenge or envy of others regardless of the circumstances. God is our reward and encouragement.

———————◆———————

But God heard the boy crying, and the angel of God called to Hagar from heaven, "Hagar, what's wrong? **Do not be afraid**! God has heard the boy crying as he lies there. Go to him and comfort him, for I will make a great nation from his descendants." Then God opened Hagar's eyes, and she saw a well full of water. She quickly filled her water container and gave the boy a drink.

Genesis 21:17-19 (NLT)

God's willingness and readiness to help in times of trouble is an encouragement for us to turn to Him for help in all things. Do not be in anguish, but allow God to open your eyes to the comfort that awaits you.

The LORD appeared to him the same night and said, "I am the God of your father Abraham; **Do not fear**, for I am with you I will bless you, and multiply your descendants, For the sake of My servant Abraham."

Genesis 26:24 (NASB)

God is faithful and gracious to provide comfort in our fear and disappointment.

———◆———

And when her labor was at its hardest, the midwife said to her, "**Do not fear**, for you have another son."

Genesis 35:17 (ESV)

Though pain and sorrows exist, we can endure knowing that a reward awaits us. As children of God we take comfort in being absolved with eternal salvation and look forward to what lay ahead without fear.

The servant said, Don't worry. **Don't be afraid**. Your God, the God of your father, must have put the money in your sacks for you. I received your payment. Then he brought Simeon to them.

Genesis 43:23 (GNT)

We are indebted to God for all of our happiness and blessings and for the compassion and generosity of our friends. Do not be afraid or ask how or why; accept it as divine guidance.

———————◆———————

He said, "I am God, the God of your father; **do not be afraid** to go down to Egypt, for I will make you a great nation there. I will go down with you to Egypt, and I will also surely bring you up again; and Joseph will close your eyes."

Genesis 46:3-4 (NASB)

Our fears are silenced knowing that wherever God sends us, we are assured that He will also be with us.

But Joseph replied, "**Don't be afraid** of me. Am I God, that I can punish you? You intended to harm me, but God intended it all for good. He brought me to this position so I could save the lives of many people."

Genesis 50:19-20 (NLT)

When we ask forgiveness from someone we have offended, do not place them in such high a position that we are afraid of their disapproval. Make peace with God and you will find it easier to make peace with man.

———————◆———————

"You have **nothing to fear**. I will take care of you and your children." So he reassured them with kind words that touched their hearts.

Genesis 50:21 (GNT)

A broken spirit must be bound up, an offer of forgiveness and a comforting word provides encouragement and comfort to drive away fear.

But Moses told the people, "**Don't be afraid**. Just stand still and watch the LORD rescue you today. The Egyptians you see today will never be seen again."

Exodus 14:13 (NLT)

In times of difficulty keep your spirits calm, so that you may be prepared to follow God's lead in doing His work as well as your own.

———◆———

Moses spoke to the people: "**Don't be afraid**. God has come to test you and instill a deep and reverent awe within you so that you won't sin."

Exodus 20:20 (MSG)

Do not allow the influence of the devil to come between you and God. Have a humble and sincere reverence of His majesty, be obedient to His authority and dread His displeasure. Stand in awe of Him to be motivated and attentive in your walk.

———◆———

Be honest and just when you make decisions in legal cases; **do not** show favoritism to the poor or **fear the rich**.

Leviticus 19:15 (GNT)

Wisdom permits us to discern the truth which allows us to become fearless to intimidation.

I will give you peace in the land, and you will be able to sleep with **no cause for fear**. I will rid the land of wild animals and keep your enemies out of your land.

Leviticus 26:6 (NLT)

We are saved by the power and promises of God, let His peace replace your fear and worry and keep you safe.

———◆———

Do not rebel against the LORD, and **don't be afraid** of the people of the land. They are only helpless prey to us! They have no protection, but the LORD is with us! **Don't be afraid** of them!

Numbers 14:9 (NLT)

No matter how tough things appear do not be afraid or lose faith, for God is with you.

———◆———

But the LORD said to Moses, "**Do not fear** him, for I have given him into your hand, and all his people and his land; and you shall do to him as you did to Sihon, king of the Amorites, who lived at Heshbon."

Numbers 21:34 (NASB)

The stronghold of fear is no match against the judgment of God. Let each victory be an encouragement to us.

Do not show partiality in judging; hear both small and great alike. **Do not be afraid** of any man, for judgment belongs to God. Bring me any case too hard for you, and I will hear it.

Deuteronomy 1:17 (NIV)

Do not fear others when making righteous choices or decisions, regardless of what others may think or say.

————◆————

See, the LORD your God has given you the land. Go up and take possession of it as the LORD, the God of your fathers, told you. **Do not be afraid**; do not be discouraged."

Deuteronomy 1:21 (NIV)

Be strong and follow the promptings of God, otherwise you risk missing out on His blessing.

"Where can we go? Our brothers have made our hearts melt in fear. They say, 'The people are stronger and taller than we are; the cities are large, with walls up to the sky. We even saw the Anakites there.'" Then I said to you, "Do not be terrified; **do not be afraid** of them. The LORD your God, who is going before you, will fight for you, as he did for you in Egypt, before your very eyes, and in the wilderness. There you saw how the LORD your God carried you, as a father carries his son, all the way you went until you reached this place."

Deuteronomy 1:28-31 (TNIV)

When we recall previous blessings from God our strength and confidence are built up and we are able to step out in faith to overcome unfounded fear.

———————◆———————

And the Lord said to me, **Do not fear** him, for I have given him and all his people and his land into your hand; and you shall do to him as you did to Sihon king of the Amorites, who lived at Heshbon.

Deuteronomy 3:2 (AMP)

Be encouraged by previous victories over fear in order to build up your confidence to trust in Him the next time, for God is God.

I commanded Joshua at that time, "You've seen with your own two eyes everything God, your God, has done to these two kings. God is going to do the same thing to all the kingdoms over there across the river where you're headed. **Don't be afraid** of them. God, your God—he's fighting for you."

Deuteronomy 3:21-22 (MSG)

Confidence comes through experience, let those with experience be an encouragement to those just setting out so that they may grow strong and rely on the divine wisdom, power and goodness of God.

———————◆———————

You're going to think to yourselves, "Oh! We're outnumbered ten to one by these nations! We'll never even make a dent in them!" But I'm telling you, **Don't be afraid**. Remember, yes, remember in detail what GOD, your God, did to Pharaoh and all Egypt. Remember the great contests to which you were eyewitnesses: the miracle-signs, the wonders, God's mighty hand as he stretched out his arm and took you out of there. God, your God, is going to do the same thing to these people you're now so afraid of.

Deuteronomy 7:17-19 (MSG)

Do not be afraid or discouraged when things appear impossible, for we have God on our side. Be encouraged by recalling how God has always been on our side.

No, **do not be afraid** of those nations, for the Lord your God is among you, and he is a great and awesome God.

Deuteronomy 7:21 (NLT)

We are encouraged because God is with us. If God is with us, we have no reason to fear.

———◆———

If a prophet speaks in the name of the LORD and what he says does not come true, then it is not the LORD's message. That prophet has spoken on his own authority, and you are **not to fear** him.

Deuteronomy 18:22 (GNT)

Do not be misled by those that would spread fear.

———◆———

When you go out to battle against your enemies and see horses and chariots and people more numerous than you, **do not be afraid** of them; for the LORD your God, who brought you up from the land of Egypt, is with you.

Deuteronomy 20:1 (NASB)

God is with us; He is our protector no matter how bleak or impossible things may appear. Where would we be without Him? Let Him be your confidence.

'Men of Israel, listen! Today you are going into battle. **Do not be afraid** of your enemies or lose courage or panic. The Lord your God is going with you, and he will give you victory.'

Deuteronomy 20:3-4 (GNT)

Have confidence and faith in the power and promises of God. He is with you to provide victory for your righteous cause.

———————◆———————

The officers will continue, "**Is any man afraid?** Is anyone scared? Let him go home. Then the other men won't lose hope too."

Deuteronomy 20:8 (NIrV)

Fear can be contagious like a virus, but God can strengthen and protect us from its spread. Do not allow the fear of those who are afraid infect you.

———————◆———————

"Be strong and courageous, **do not be afraid** or tremble at them, for the LORD your God is the one who goes with you He will not fail you or forsake you."

Deuteronomy 31:6 (NASB)

Because we have the power of God on our side we have no reason to fear.

Then Moses called to Joshua and said to him in the sight of all Israel, "Be strong and courageous, for you shall go with this people into the land which the LORD has sworn to their fathers to give them, and you shall give it to them as an inheritance. The LORD is the one who goes ahead of you; He will be with you He will not fail you or forsake you. **Do not fear** or be dismayed."

Deuteronomy 31:7-8 (NASB)

God is faithful to His promises. Be strong and courageous knowing that God is with us, for when God is with us leading the charge fear flees in retreat.

———————◆———————

"This is my command—be strong and courageous! **Do not be afraid** or discouraged. For the LORD your God is with you wherever you go."

Joshua 1:9 (NLT)

It is God's will for us to stand up to fear, which is the root of doubt and discouragement.

Then the LORD said to Joshua, "**Do not be afraid**; do not be discouraged. Take the whole army with you, and go up and attack Ai. For I have delivered into your hands the king of Ai, his people, his city and his land."

Joshua 8:1 (NIV)

Faithful repentance leads to expectant comfort from God who is able to deliver us from fear and discouragement.

◆

The LORD said to Joshua, "**Do not fear** them, for I have given them into your hands; not one of them shall stand before you."

Joshua 10:8 (NASB)

God delivers us from hopelessness and renders fear powerless.

◆

"**Don't ever be afraid** or discouraged," Joshua told his men. "Be strong and courageous, for the LORD is going to do this to all of your enemies."

Joshua 10:25 (NLT)

We have victory over fear through Christ who has already defeated the enemy.

But the Lord said to Joshua, **Do not be afraid** because of them, for tomorrow by this time I will give them up all slain to Israel; you shall hamstring their horses and burn their chariots with fire.

Joshua 11:6 (AMP)

God is able to stop fear in its tracks; He proportions our strength to our fear so that we can trample over it victoriously.

———◆———

Meanwhile Sisera, running for his life, headed for the tent of Jael, wife of Heber the Kenite. Jabin king of Hazor and Heber the Kenite were on good terms with one another. Jael stepped out to meet Sisera and said, "Come in, sir. Stay here with me. **Don't be afraid**." So he went with her into her tent. She covered him with a blanket.

Judges 4:17-18 (MSG)

Self confidence and misguided trust results in a false sense of security, faith and trust in God provides authentic eternal security.

When Gideon saw that he was the angel of the LORD, he said, "Alas, O Lord GOD! For now I have seen the angel of the LORD face to face." The LORD said to him, "Peace to you, **do not fear**; you shall not die."

Judges 6:22-23 (NASB)

God encourages hearts that are filled with worship; we stand in awe of His majesty and assurance.

———————◆———————

And now, my daughter, **don't be afraid**. I will do for you all you ask. All the people of my town know that you are a woman of noble character.

Ruth 3:11 (TNIV)

Humility is honorable to God. When we honor Him we have no reason to be afraid, He is able to bless and reward, He is our hope.

Samuel said to the people, "**Do not fear.** You have committed all this evil, yet do not turn aside from following the LORD, but serve the LORD with all your heart."

1 Samuel 12:20 (NASB)

God did not choose us based on our good merits, had He done so we might fear He would abandon us for our bad merits. Though our evil choices displease Him, He will not abandon His covenant, so do not abandon your hope in His mercy. He is able to use all things for His good.

———◆———

David said to Saul, Your Majesty, **no one should be afraid of this Philistine**! I will go and fight him. I have killed lions and bears, and I will do the same to this heathen Philistine, who has defied the army of the living God. The Lord has saved me from lions and bears; he will save me from this Philistine.

1 Samuel 17:32, 36-37 (GNT)

Our previous experiences in trusting God are an encouragement that prepares us when undertaking new battles for Him.

So it was, when the Philistine arose and came and drew near to meet David, that David hurried and **ran toward the army** to meet the Philistine. Then David put his hand in his bag and took out a stone; and he slung it and struck the Philistine in his forehead, so that the stone sank into his forehead, and he fell on his face to the earth. So David prevailed over the Philistine with a sling and a stone, and struck the Philistine and killed him. But there was no sword in the hand of David.

1 Samuel 17:48-50 (NKJV)

Do not be afraid of the arrogant that ridicule you because of your faith, but have confidence in the promptings of the spirit. By divine guidance and determination fear is slayed!

———————◆———————

Stay with me; **do not fear**. For he who seeks my life seeks your life, but with me you shall be safe.

1 Samuel 22:23 (NKJV)

Regardless of the daily distractions of life, set aside time to be in communion with God, who provides safety and comfort.

Jonathan went to find David and encouraged him to stay strong in his faith in God. "**Don't be afraid**," Jonathan reassured him. "My father will never find you! You are going to be the king of Israel, and I will be next to you, as my father, Saul, is well aware." So the two of them renewed their solemn pact before the LORD.

1 Samuel 23:16-18a (NLT)

Direct your heart to God, who provides confidence and comfort. Be strengthened by reminding yourself of God's goodness and promises.

The king told her, "You have **nothing to fear** ...but what do you see?" "I see a spirit ascending from the underground."

1 Samuel 28:13 (MSG)

When we worship the Lord and seek His truth, deception and lies are exposed giving us confidence to press on undaunted.

"Don't be afraid," David said to him, "for I will surely show you kindness for the sake of your father Jonathan. I will restore to you all the land that belonged to your grandfather Saul, and you will always eat at my table."

2 Samuel 9:7 (NIV)

Do not be afraid to approach those in a position of higher authority than you. In the same way encourage those that you may have authority over, as God encourages us to approach Him.

————◆————

But Elijah said to her, **"Don't be afraid!** Go ahead and do just what you've said, but make a little bread for me first. Then use what's left to prepare a meal for yourself and your son. For this is what the LORD, the God of Israel, says: There will always be flour and olive oil left in your containers until the time when the LORD sends rain and the crops grow again!" So she did as Elijah said, and she and Elijah and her son continued to eat for many days. There was always enough flour and olive oil left in the containers, just as the LORD had promised through Elijah.

1 Kings 17:13-16 (NLT)

Those that have trust and confidence in the promises of God have no worries when it comes to giving of them selves in service to God. Trust God, seek first His kingdom, then other things will be added.

The angel of GOD told Elijah, "Go ahead; and **don't be afraid**." Elijah got up and went down with him to the king.

2 Kings 1:15 (MSG)

Do not allow fear to hold you back from boldly speaking the truth.

———————◆———————

When the servant of the man of God got up early the next morning and went outside, there were troops, horses, and chariots everywhere. "Oh, sir, what will we do now?" the young man cried to Elisha. "**Don't be afraid!**" Elisha told him. "For there are more on our side than on theirs!" Then Elisha prayed, "O LORD, open his eyes and let him see!" The LORD opened the young man's eyes, and when he looked up, he saw that the hillside around Elisha was filled with horses and chariots of fire.

2 Kings 6:15-17 (NLT)

Do not make things out to be worse than they are; turn to God so that our eyes are open to see things as they really are. God is larger than anything.

Isaiah said to them, "Thus you shall say to your master, 'Thus says the LORD, "**Do not be afraid** because of the words that you have heard, with which the servants of the king of Assyria have blasphemed Me. Behold, I will put a spirit in him so that he will hear a rumor and return to his own land And I will make him fall by the sword in his own land."'"

2 Kings 19:6-7 (NASB)

God is able to extinguish the pain of hurtful words and drive away the source of fear.

———————◆———————

Gedaliah assured the officers and their men, giving them his word, "**Don't be afraid** of the Babylonian officials. Go back to your farms and families and respect the king of Babylon. Trust me, everything is going to be all right."

2 Kings 25:24 (MSG)

Don't be blinded by unfounded fears. Be satisfied with what you have and know that we have an eternal hope.

I have given my people Israel a land of their own where they can live in peace. They will **no longer have to tremble with fear**—evil nations won't bother them, as they did when I let judges rule my people, and I will keep your enemies from attacking you. Now I promise that like you, your descendants will be kings.

1 Chronicles 17:9-10 (CEV)

God is our protector and provider, let Him be your place of peace and comfort, He keeps the enemy of fear from attacking.

————◆————

Only, may the LORD grant you discretion and understanding, that when he gives you charge over Israel you may keep the law of the LORD your God. Then you will prosper if you are careful to observe the statutes and the rules that the LORD commanded Moses for Israel. Be strong and courageous. **Fear not**; do not be dismayed.

1 Chronicles 22:12-13 (ESV)

Look to God for discretion and understanding in whatever work He has called you to. Press on without fear regardless of how large or small the task may seem. Gods work will always be completed.

Then David said to Solomon his son, "Be strong and courageous and do it. **Do not be afraid** and do not be dismayed, for the LORD God, even my God, is with you. He will not leave you or forsake you, until all the work for the service of the house of the LORD is finished."

1 Chronicles 28:20 (ESV)

In serving God, do not fear the task, do not fear the opposition, do not fear its completion. Look to God first, He will be your strength and helper. Nothing is too big for Him.

———————◆———————

He said, "Listen, all you people of Judah and Jerusalem! Listen, King Jehoshaphat! This is what the LORD says: **Do not be afraid!** Don't be discouraged by this mighty army, for the battle is not yours, but God's."

2 Chronicles 20:15 (NLT)

We are drawn to the feet of the Father when the enemy of fear threatens. Take courage and allow God to be God in your life for the battle belongs to the Lord.

"'You will not need to fight in this battle. Stand firm, hold your position, and see the salvation of the LORD on your behalf, O Judah and Jerusalem.' **Do not be afraid** and do not be dismayed. Tomorrow go out against them, and the LORD will be with you."

2 Chronicles 20:17 (ESV)

Do not let fear get the best of you, stand firm in your faith and witness God's victory over fear.

———◆———

Be strong and courageous, **do not fear** or be dismayed because of the king of Assyria nor because of all the horde that is with him; for the one with us is greater than the one with him.

2 Chronicles 32:7 (NASB)

Be confident in the word of God and rise above fear. With boldness we declare that since God is for us, who can be against us?

After I looked things over, I stood up and said to the nobles, the officials and the rest of the people, **"Don't be afraid** of them. Remember the Lord, who is great and awesome, and fight for your people, your sons and your daughters, your wives and your homes." When our enemies heard that we were aware of their plot and that God had frustrated it, we all returned to the wall, each to our own work.

Nehemiah 4:14-15 (TNIV)

Fear is an enemy that deceives, with God as our leader we are made strong and able to go on with His work. Through prayer and vigilance we are able to stand up for all that is right and all that we cherish.

———◆———

Our enemies were trying to frighten us and to keep us from our work. But I asked God to give me strength.

Nehemiah 6:9 (CEV)

Lift up faithful prayers to God for the courage and determination to press on through fear and temptation. Our character is strengthened when we face our fears.

When there isn't enough food, God will keep you
from dying. When you go into battle, he won't let a
sword strike you down. He will keep you safe from
words that can hurt you. You **won't need to be afraid**
when everything is being destroyed.

Job 5:20-21 (NIrV)

We have holy security and confidence because of
our hope in God's protection and provision.

————◆————

You will laugh when things are being destroyed.
You will enjoy life even when there isn't enough food.
You **won't be afraid** of wild animals. You will make a
covenant with the stones in the fields. They won't keep
your crops from growing. Even wild animals will be at
peace with you.

Job 5:22-23 (NIrV)

Though we may stumble we need not be afraid, for
we have a peace that allows us to be encouraged by the
power and greatness of God, even during trials.

So commit yourself to God completely. Reach out your hands to him for help. Get rid of all of the sin you have. Don't let anything that is evil stay in your tent. Then you can face others without feeling any shame. You can stand firm **without being afraid**.

Job 11:13-15 (NIrV)

Set your heart on God and reach out to Him with the full assurance of faith that we are washed with the blood of Christ. The more we fix ourselves on Him, the less we have to fear.

———————◆———————

You will rest safe and secure, filled with hope and emptied of worry. You will **sleep without fear** and be greatly respected.

Job 11:18-19 (CEV)

Hope is a pillar of the soul. Those with hope in God, through grace, have no reason to worry or be afraid.

We each were made from clay, and God has no favorites, so **don't be afraid** of me or what I might do.

Job 33:6-7 (CEV)

We have no reason to fear a man, for we are all formed the same way. We are like clay pots molded by the cracks of life. May the light of Jesus shine brightly through our cracks!

———————◆———————

Before horses are ridden into battle, they paw at the ground, proud of their strength. **Laughing at fear,** they rush toward the fighting, while the weapons of their riders rattle and flash in the sun. Unable to stand still, they gallop eagerly into battle when trumpets blast.

Job 39:21-24 (CEV)

Undaunted by what lies ahead we eagerly press on with fearless courage.

I lie down and sleep, and all night long the Lord protects me. **I am not afraid** of the thousands of enemies who surround me on every side.

Psalm 3:5-6 (GNT)

Regardless of criticism, intimidation and judgment from man, we commit ourselves to God and depend on His blessings. Our confidence in Him is built up through submission to Him.

———◆———

I will always look to you, as you stand beside me and **protect me from fear**.

Psalm 16:8 (CEV)

We are able to persevere against fear because God is by our side; we turn to Him for protection.

———◆———

I may walk through valleys as dark as death, but I **won't be afraid**. You are with me, and your shepherd's rod makes me feel safe.

Psalm 23:4 (CEV)

Christ is our shepherd that comforts, protects and guides us through the darkest times. We have nothing to fear because nothing can separate us from God's love.

The LORD is my light and my salvation; **whom shall I fear**? the LORD is the strength of my life; of **whom shall I be afraid?**

Psalm 27:1 (KJV)

Have no fear of any man. The light of the Lord shines the way for us when we are confused and apprehensive; through Him we have salvation and find strength.

———◆———

I looked to the Lord, and he answered me. **He saved me from everything I was afraid of.** Those who look to him beam with joy. They are never put to shame.

Psalm 34:4-5 (NIrV)

We find comfort and joy in God through prayer; he is able to deliver us from all our fears.

Even if an army attacks me, my heart will **not be afraid**. Even if war breaks out against me, I will still trust in God.

Psalm 37:3 (NIrV)

Peace and security are found in the hearts of God's people through prayer, through His promise and by His power. He is our salvation and peace that is able to remove fear.

———◆———

God is our refuge and strength, always ready to help in times of trouble. So **we will not fear** when earthquakes come and the mountains crumble into the sea.

Psalm 46:1-2 (NLT)

When worry and fear abound God is our safe refuge. Even when our world seems upside down He is our strong rock.

I am **not afraid** in times of danger when I am surrounded by enemies, by evil people who trust in their riches and boast of their great wealth.

Psalm 49:5-6 (GNT)

There is no reason to be afraid of people, even those with affluence and wealth, they have no power. When judgment comes, those who put their hope in the wealth of the world will be afraid, but those who trust in the Lord will be safe.

———————◆———————

Do not be afraid when a man becomes rich, When the glory of his house is increased; For when he dies he will carry nothing away; His glory will not descend after him.

Psalm 49:16-17 (NASB)

Do not be envious or fearful of those with worldly riches and power, for the wealth of this world does not pass on to the next. Remember that we all enter the world as sinful people, but believers exit the world, through grace, renewed and covered in the richness and righteousness of Christ.

By [the help of] God I will praise His word; on God I lean, rely, and confidently put my trust; I **will not fear**. What can man, who is flesh, do to me?

Psalm 56:4 (AMP)

When we are afraid we can place our trust and confidence in God and praise Him for His promises. Do not fear what man can do because men can only do what God permits. When we put our trust in God, He is glorified.

———————◆———————

In God have I put my trust: I will **not be afraid** what man can do unto me.

Psalm 56:11 (KJV)

Believers know that man has no power except that which God has given him. When we trust in the promises of God we are not afraid.

But he led his own people like a flock of sheep, guiding them safely through the wilderness. He kept them safe so they **were not afraid**; but the sea covered their enemies.

Psalm 78:52-53 (NLT)

When our paths seem dark and dangerous God is able to lead us through them safely. God can use the same path that leads us to safety to conquer our enemies.

————◆————

Do not be afraid of the terrors of the night, nor the arrow that flies in the day. Do not dread the disease that stalks in darkness, nor the disaster that strikes at midday.

Psalm 91:5-6 (NLT)

When terror strikes, it is enough to frighten us night and day, but by God's grace we have His promise of security to save us from its grip.

He is not afraid of receiving bad news; his faith is strong, and he trusts in the LORD.

Psalm 112:7 (GNT)

Our responsibility as believers is to not be afraid of or dwell on bad news, rumors or gossip which only serves to frustrate, but to have a heart that is grounded in faith with complete confidence and trust in God.

———◆———

He is not worried or **afraid**; he is certain to see his enemies defeated.

Psalm 112:8 (GNT)

Even though we may experience troubles and adversity we will not be afraid, for we know that the Lord is able to deliver us and that our spiritual enemies are destined for defeat.

I love the Lord, because he hears me; he listens to my prayers. He listens to me every time I call to him. The danger of death was all around me; the horrors of the grave closed in on me; **I was filled with fear** and anxiety. Then I called to the Lord, I beg you, Lord, save me!

Psalm 116:1-4 (GNT)

When it seems like you are at the end of your rope, do not allow fear and anxiousness to get the best of you as it only serves to compound issues. God loves to hear from us, so turn to Him in faithful prayer and place yourself under His protection, let prayer be your first resort... not your last.

———————◆———————

The Lord saved me from death; he stopped my tears and kept me from defeat. And so I walk in the presence of the Lord in the world of the living. I kept on believing, even when I said, "I am completely crushed," even **when I was afraid** and said, "No one can be trusted."

Psalm 116:8-11 (GNT)

Fear can cause us to make decisions in haste, place your faith and trust in the promises of the Lord, not in man, and keep on believing.

The LORD is on my side; **I will not fear**: what can man do unto me?

Psalm 118:6 (KJV)

If we are on God's side, then we have no need to be afraid, for He is with us. If God is with us then, who can be against us!

———◆———

Keep your promise to me, your servant—the promise you make to those who obey you. Save me from the insults **I fear**; how wonderful are your judgments! I want to obey your commands; give me new life, for you are righteous.

Psalm 119:38-40 (GNT)

The criticism we receive from man cannot compare to the judgment of the Lord, but it can harm our Christian witness and reputation. We pray that God would use the contempt of men for the sake of His witness and give us the desire to know Him more.

"But whoever listens to me will have security. He will be safe, with **no reason to be afraid**."

Proverbs 1:33 (GNT)

When we seek and follow the counsel of God we are assured of being safe from evil and have no reason to fear it.

————◆————

My child, hold on to your wisdom and insight. Never let them get away from you. They will provide you with life—a pleasant and happy life. You can go safely on your way and never even stumble. You will **not be afraid** when you go to bed, and you will sleep soundly through the night.

Proverbs 3:21-24 (GNT)

Wisdom guides us through life, keeps us from temptation so that we can walk in confidence and without fear. We are protected by the one that never sleeps.

Be not afraid of sudden terror and panic, nor of the stormy blast or the storm and ruin of the wicked when it comes [for you will be guiltless], For the Lord shall be your confidence, firm and strong, and shall keep your foot from being caught [in a trap or some hidden danger].

Proverbs 3:25-26 (AMP)

When you are caught off guard and become confused, never lose sight of the Lord who is our protector, let Him be your confidence.

————◆————

If you are afraid of people, it will trap you. But if you trust in the Lord, he will keep you safe.

Proverbs 29:25 (NIrV)

Do not hesitate from your responsibilities in order to avoid trouble or temptation from man. Depend on the power of God whom you can trust.

Tell Ahaz, 'Be careful. Be calm and don't worry. Don't let those two men, Rezin and Pekah son of Remaliah, scare you. **Don't be afraid** of their anger or Aram's anger, because they are like two barely burning sticks that are ready to go out. They have made plans against you, saying, "Let's fight against Judah and tear it apart. We will divide the land for ourselves and make the son of Tabeel the new king of Judah." But I, the Lord God, say, "Their plan will not succeed; it will not happen,"'

Isaiah 7:4-7 (NCV)

Do not let the anger of those that are against God cause you to be afraid or worry, their threats are ultimately snuffed out. God is our consuming fire that is able to extinguish fear and worry.

With his great power the LORD warned me not to follow the road which the people were following. He said, "Do not join in the schemes of the people and **do not be afraid** of the things that they fear. Remember that I, the LORD Almighty, am holy; I am the one you must fear."

Isaiah 8:11-13 (GNT)

The Lord is our Maker, make Him the object of your fear and stand in awe of His supreme power, which overshadows the fear of our enemies.

So this is what the Lord, the LORD of Heaven's Armies, says: "O my people in Zion, **do not be afraid** of the Assyrians when they oppress you with rod and club as the Egyptians did long ago. In a little while my anger against you will end, and then my anger will rise up to destroy them."

Isaiah 10:24-25 (NLT)

Be encouraged and give thanks for Gods forgiving comfort, for the sources of our fear are ultimately crushed. We have no need to fear anything that can do no more than frighten us.

———————◆———————

Behold, God is my salvation; I will trust, and **not be afraid**: for the LORD JEHOVAH is my strength and my song; he also is become my salvation.

Isaiah 12:2 (KJV)

God is our strength and confidence; we give thankful praises and look to Him for comfort during times of trouble.

With this news, strengthen those who have tired hands, and encourage those who have weak knees. Say to those with fearful hearts, "Be strong, and **do not fear**, for your God is coming to destroy your enemies. He is coming to save you."

Isaiah 35:3-4 (NLT)

Let God be our encouragement to press against fear, which only seeks to weaken us. The more we press on and endure the more our fears are silenced and the stronger we become.

———————◆———————

he said to them, "Tell your master this: The Lord says, **'Don't be afraid** of what you have heard. **Don't be frightened** by the words the servants of the king of Assyria have spoken against me. Listen! I am going to put a spirit in the king of Assyria. He will hear a report that will make him return to his own country, and I will cause him to die by the sword there.'"

Isaiah 37:6-7 (NCV)

Those that belong to God have no reason to fear those that are against Him. Though enemies may make fun of and mock, they cannot hurt. God will ultimately judge.

O Zion, messenger of good news, shout from the mountaintops! Shout it louder, O Jerusalem. Shout, and **do not be afraid**. Tell the towns of Judah, "Your God is coming!" Yes, the Sovereign LORD is coming in power. He will rule with a powerful arm. See, he brings his reward with him as he comes. He will feed his flock like a shepherd. He will carry the lambs in his arms, holding them close to his heart. He will gently lead the mother sheep with their young.

Isaiah 40:9-11 (NLT)

God is our redeemer and our reward, do not be afraid to speak it loudly and boldly, for He cares for and loves those that are His.

———————◆———————

So **do not fear**, for I am with you; do not be dismayed, for I am your God. I will strengthen you and help you; I will uphold you with my righteous right hand.

Isaiah 41:10 (NIV)

God does not want us to be afraid of threats or to doubt His promises. He assures us of deliverance to strengthen our faith. He is with us in our weakness.

For I am the LORD your God, who upholds your right hand, Who says to you, **'Do not fear**, I will help you.'

Isaiah 41:13 (NASB)

Have no fear, for God walks hand in hand with us. He is our guide and encourager, able to help when we fall.

———————◆———————

The Lord says, Small and weak as you are, Israel, **don't be afraid**; I will help you. I, the holy God of Israel, am the one who saves you.

Isaiah 41:14 (GNT)

Help is found in Christ who redeems us, even when we are overwhelmed. God's grace can silence your fears.

———————◆———————

But now, this is what the LORD says—he who created you, O Jacob, he who formed you, O Israel: "**Fear not**, for I have redeemed you; I have summoned you by name; you are mine."

Isaiah 43:1 (NIV)

Rejoice in God's mercy and goodness for it sustains us. We take comfort in Him and are not afraid, for He chose us, we are His.

Do not fear, for I am with you; I will bring your offspring from the east, And gather you from the west.

Isaiah 43:5 (NASB)

We are the church created for His glory; we are bound together with Christ and have nothing to fear.

————◆————

The LORD who made you and helps you says: **Do not be afraid**, O Jacob, my servant, O dear Israel, my chosen one.

Isaiah 44:2 (NLT)

God chose us as His servants, for this reason we are not afraid. When we serve Him we fall under His protection.

————◆————

"**Do not be afraid**, my people! You know that from ancient times until now I have predicted all that would happen, and you are my witnesses. Is there any other god? Is there some powerful god I never heard of"

Isaiah 44:8 (GNT)

Do not be afraid of what you witness in the world or things you have no control over. We can depend on His promises, He is in control. He is to be worshipped!

Listen to Me, you who know rightness and justice and right standing with God, the people in whose heart is My law and My instruction: **fear not** the reproach of men, **neither be afraid** nor dismayed at their revilings. For [in comparison with the Lord they are so weak that things as insignificant as] the moth shall eat them up like a garment, and the worm shall eat them like wool. But My rightness and justice [and faithfully fulfilled promise] shall be forever, and My salvation to all generations.

Isaiah 51:7-8 (AMP)

Do not be afraid of the contempt, lies and disapproval of men, for they will be silenced and the truth will be celebrated.

———————◆———————

The Lord says to his people, "I comfort you because of who I am. **Why are you afraid** of mere men? They are only human beings. They are like grass that dries up."

Isaiah 51:12 (NIrV)

Do not fear the scorn of men, but run to God who provides comfort. The fact that God Himself would even provide comfort is comforting in itself.

Have you forgotten the Lord who made you, who stretched out the heavens and laid the earth's foundations? **Why should you live in constant fear** of the fury of those who oppress you, of those who are ready to destroy you? Their fury can no longer touch you.

Isaiah 51:13 (GNT)

Do not be a slave to the fear of men, for man has no power but that which God allows. Keep in mind that God is the designer of all creation and the one to be feared and worshiped.

———◆———

Don't be afraid or ashamed and don't be discouraged. You won't be disappointed. Forget how sinful you were when you were young; stop feeling ashamed for being left a widow. The LORD All-Powerful, the Holy God of Israel, rules all the earth. He is your Creator and husband, and he will rescue you.

Isaiah 54:4-5 (CEV)

Do not be afraid or ashamed of your previous life, the life before you was redeemed from the enslavement of sin by Christ.

When you do what is right, you will be made secure. Your leaders will not be mean to you. **You will not have anything to be afraid of.** You will **not be terrified** anymore. Terror will not come near you.

Isaiah 54:14 (NIrV)

When the Lord reigns in your life evil oppression is put in its place and we are free of fear.

———◆———

"**Do not be afraid** of them, For I am with you to deliver you," declares the LORD.

Jeremiah 1:8 (NASB)

God is with us, we have no reason to fear the disapproval or concern of man.

———◆———

Get up and prepare for action. Go out and tell them everything I tell you to say. **Do not be afraid** of them, or I will make you look foolish in front of them.

Jeremiah 1:17 (NLT)

The fear of God is the best method to counteract the fear of man. Let us worship Him.

This is what the Lord says: "Do not act like the other nations, who try to read their future in the stars. **Do not be afraid** of their predictions, even though other nations are terrified by them. Their ways are futile and foolish. They cut down a tree, and a craftsman carves an idol."

Jeremiah 10:2-3 (NLT)

Do not fear or conform to the practices of astrologers or to those who worship anyone or anything other than God. Do not be afraid of anything just because others are afraid.

———————◆———————

[Most] blessed is the man who believes in, trusts in, and relies on the Lord, and whose hope and confidence the Lord is. For he shall be like a tree planted by the waters that spreads out its roots by the river; and it **shall not** see and **fear** when heat comes; but its leaf shall be green. It shall not be anxious and full of care in the year of drought, nor shall it cease yielding fruit.

Jeremiah 17:7-8 (AMP)

God is our hope, we trust in His power and strength to carry us during times of drought. We will not worry or be afraid for He is our fountain providing us with inward peace and satisfaction.

I will bring the rest of my people home from the lands where I have scattered them, and they will grow into a mighty nation. I promise to choose leaders who will care for them like real shepherds. All of my people will be there, and they will **never again be frightened**.

Jeremiah 23:3-4 (CEV)

Though we were lost and afraid, we are now confident and rejoice in Gods mercy to gather His church.

———————◆———————

'So **do not fear**, O Jacob my servant; do not be dismayed, O Israel,' declares the LORD. 'I will surely save you out of a distant place, your descendants from the land of their exile. Jacob will again have peace and security, and **no one will make him afraid**. I am with you and will save you,' declares the LORD.

Jeremiah 30:10-11a (NIV)

The promises of God are enough to extinguish fear and grief, we will not surrender to difficulties or troubles that threaten us, but will turn to God for the security that only He can provide.

But I will deliver you on that day, declares the LORD, and you shall **not be given into the hand of the men of whom you are afraid**.

Jeremiah 39:17 (ESV)

God knows our fears, when we trust in Him we have confidence in His promise of deliverance and have no need to fear any man.

———————◆———————

Gedaliah son of Ahikam, the son of Shaphan, took an oath to give hope to all of those men. He spoke in a kind way to them. He said, "**Don't be afraid** to serve the Babylonians. Settle down in the land of Judah. Serve the king of Babylonia. Then things will go well with you."

Jeremiah 40:9 (NIrV)

We will not be afraid of criticism or the stigma associated with our current circumstances, for God is with us, He is in control.

Be not afraid of the king of Babylon, of whom ye are afraid; **be not afraid** of him, saith the LORD: for I am with you to save you, and to deliver you from his hand.

Jeremiah 42:11 (KJV)

Do not be discouraged or afraid of obstacles you perceive as insurmountable, but abide in the safety of God's promises that will deliver you.

———————◆———————

My people, **do not be afraid**, people of Israel, do not be terrified. I will rescue you from that faraway land, from the land where you are prisoners. You will come back home and live in peace; you will be secure, and **no one will make you afraid**.

Jeremiah 46:27 (GNT)

God's mercy carries us through difficulties. We put our hope in His promises and will not fear.

So **don't be afraid**, even though now you deserve
to be punished and have been scattered among other
nations. But when I destroy them, I will protect you. I,
the LORD, have spoken.

Jeremiah 46:28 (CEV)

We trust in the faithfulness of God to protect us.
We are at home in Him, for if God is with us who can
be against us.

———◆———

Come out of there, my people! Run for your lives!
Run away from my burning anger. You will hear about
terrible things that are happening in Babylonia. But do
not lose hope. **Do not be afraid**. You will hear one
thing this year. And you will hear something else next
year. You will hear about awful things in the land. You
will hear about one ruler fighting against another.

Jeremiah 51:45-46 (NIrV)

Do not let fear and temptation, or the threat of it,
be a burden to you, flee from it. Put fear to rest through
faith in God's promises.

I called on your name, O LORD, from the depths of the pit. You heard my plea: "Do not close your ears to my cry for relief." You came near when I called you, and you said, "**Do not fear.**" O Lord, you took up my case; you redeemed my life.

Lamentations 3:55-58 (NIV)

By faith we can always count on Gods ear and grace to quiet our fear.

And you, son of man, **be not afraid** of them, **neither be afraid** of their words; though briers and thorns are all around you and you dwell and sit among scorpions, **be not afraid** of their words nor be dismayed at their looks, for they are a rebellious house. And you shall speak My words to them whether they will hear or refuse to hear, for they are most rebellious.

Ezekiel 2:6-7 (AMP)

Do not be afraid to speak the truth, or be put off by the words of those that would hinder you. In uncompromising service to God, speak and act boldly with assured protection from above.

"But it won't work that way with the family of
Israel. They won't listen to you because they won't listen
to me. They are, as I said, a hard case, hardened in their
sin. But I'll make you as hard in your way as they are in
theirs. I'll make your face as hard as rock, harder than
granite. Don't let them intimidate you. **Don't be afraid**
of them, even though they're a bunch of rebels."

Ezekiel 3:7-9 (MSG)

When we follow and serve God we are assured of
His favor, and need not worry or fear the arrogance of
others. Speak firmly without fear to those requiring
correction.

———————◆———————

The trees will yield their fruit and the ground will
yield its crops; the people will be secure in their land.
They will know that I am the LORD, when I break the
bars of their yoke and rescue them from the hands of
those who enslaved them. They will no longer be
plundered by the nations, nor will wild animals devour
them. They will live in safety, and **no one will make
them afraid**.

Ezekiel 34:27-28 (TNIV)

Christ has broken the chains of sin and death and
we are secure from the evil that enslaves and from the
fear of it. In Christ we have victory.

Then he said, "**Don't be afraid**, Daniel. Since the first day you began to pray for understanding and to humble yourself before your God, your request has been heard in heaven. I have come in answer to your prayer."

Daniel 10:12 (NLT)

We are assured that our prayers are heard when offered earnestly and with humility, and are expectant and unafraid of His answer. Just as God's word is enlightening to us, know that our prayers are pleasing to Him

———◆———

"**Don't be afraid**," he said, "for you are very precious to God. Peace! Be encouraged! Be strong!" As he spoke these words to me, I suddenly felt stronger and said to him, "Please speak to me, my lord, for you have strengthened me."

Daniel 10:19 (NLT)

We are loved by God and have no reason to be afraid of any evil. His peace is our strength. May God's strength enable us to do His will!

Don't be afraid, my people. Be glad now and rejoice, for the Lord has done great things.

Joel 2:21 (NLT)

We rejoice in the faithfulness of the Lord who is able to drive our fear away.

———————◆———————

Wild animals, **don't be afraid**. The grasslands are turning green again. The trees are bearing their fruit. The vines and fig trees are producing rich crops. People of Zion, be glad. Be joyful because of what the Lord your God has done. He has given you the right amount of rain in the fall. He has sent you plenty of showers. He has sent fall and spring rains alike, just as he did before.

Joel 2:22-23 (NIrV)

We celebrate God's abundant provision and mercy which puts fear to rest. He is able to restore us.

———————◆———————

The people of Israel who survive will live right and refuse to tell lies. They will eat and rest with **nothing to fear**.

Zephaniah 3:13 (CEV)

A blessed peace surrounds those who trust in the Father and bring glory to His name. The promise of the gospel provides comfort and hope.

Sing, Jerusalem. Israel, shout for joy! Jerusalem, be happy and rejoice with all your heart. The Lord has stopped punishing you; he has sent your enemies away. The King of Israel, the Lord, is with you; you will **never again be afraid** of being harmed.

Zephaniah 3:14-15 (NCV)

Because of Christ's victory over sin we celebrate and have no worry of judgment. He is with us! There is no condemnation for those that are with Christ.

———◆———

In that day it shall be said to Jerusalem: "**Do not fear**; Zion, let not your hands be weak. The LORD your God in your midst, The Mighty One, will save; He will rejoice over you with gladness, He will quiet you with His love, He will rejoice over you with singing."

Zephaniah 3:16-17 (NKJV)

Lift your hands in praise and rejoice in the promises of God. We are not afraid because God is with us, and when God is with us no one is against us.

'As for the promise which I made you when you came out of Egypt, My Spirit is abiding in your midst; **do not fear!**'

Haggai 2:5 (NASB)

The Spirit of God is among us, we have no reason to fear or be discouraged.

———————◆———————

Judah and Israel, in the past the nations called down curses on you. But now I will save you. You will be a blessing to others. **Do not be afraid.** Let your hands be strong so that you can do my work.

Zechariah 8:13 (NIrV)

When we encounter difficulties while engaged in the work of God we can press on without fear for our reward is great.

The Lord who rules over all says, "Years ago your people made me angry. So I decided to bring trouble on them. I did not show them any pity. But now I plan to do good things to Jerusalem and Judah again. So **do not be afraid**."

Zechariah 8:14-15 (NIrV)

When we seek counsel and guidance from the Father we become fearless and are able to find comfort in His love and justice.

————◆————

And Joseph her husband, being a righteous man and not wanting to disgrace her, planned to send her away secretly. But when he had considered this, behold, an angel of the Lord appeared to him in a dream, saying, "Joseph, son of David, **do not be afraid** to take Mary as your wife; for the Child who has been conceived in her is of the Holy Spirit."

Matthew 1:19-20 (NASB)

When we quiet ourselves before God we are most receptive to His calming Spirit, who is able to deliver us from our doubts and fears.

The disciples went and woke him, saying, "Lord, save us! We're going to drown!" He replied, "You of little faith, **why are you so afraid?**" Then he got up and rebuked the winds and the waves, and it was completely calm. The men were amazed and asked, "What kind of man is this? Even the winds and the waves obey him!"

Matthew 8:25-27 (TNIV)

Christ answers the prayers of those that call Him Lord. He is able to calm our fear and strengthen our faith in the most turbulent circumstance.

———◆———

So **do not be afraid** of them. There is nothing concealed that will not be disclosed, or hidden that will not be made known.

Matthew 10:26 (NIV)

Do not be concerned for the things of this world or from what man can do, but be concerned with the condition of your soul. We worship a God that no earthly adversity or fear can separate us from.

And fear not them which kill the body, but are not able to kill the soul: but rather fear him which is able to destroy both soul and body in hell.

Matthew 10:28 (KJV)

The fear of man can be a deceptive trap that draws us into sin. Instead, have a sincere faith in Christ and never be ashamed of your relationship with Him, for those who truly worship God need not fear any man.

———————◆———————

Are not two sparrows sold for a penny? Yet not one of them will fall to the ground apart from the will of your Father. And even the very hairs of your head are all numbered. So **don't be afraid**; you are worth more than many sparrows.

Matthew 10:29-31 (NIV)

No matter what man's opinion of us is, we are valuable in the sight of God, who can silence all fears.

And when the disciples saw Him walking on the sea, they were terrified and said, It is a ghost! And they screamed out with fright. But instantly He spoke to them, saying, Take courage! I AM! **Stop being afraid!**

Matthew 14:26-27 (AMP)

The more we know Christ the more we trust Him. The storms of fear are silenced because Christ is near.

———————◆———————

"Come," Jesus said. So Peter got out of the boat. He walked on the water toward Jesus. But when Peter saw the wind, **he was afraid**. He began to sink. He cried out, "Lord! Save me!" Right away Jesus reached out his hand and caught him. "Your faith is so small!" he said. **"Why did you doubt me?"**

Matthew 14:29-31 (NIrV)

Drown out fear and doubt through strong faith in Christ, He is able to calm the winds of fear, so reach out to Him in purposeful prayer.

While Peter was still speaking, the shadow of a bright cloud passed over them. From the cloud a voice said, "This is my own dear Son, and I am pleased with him. Listen to what he says!" When the disciples heard the voice, they were so afraid that they fell flat on the ground. But Jesus came over and touched them. He said, "Get up and **don't be afraid!**"

Matthew 17:5-7 (CEV)

What a comfort it is that Christ is nearby, that through His word and touch of grace He is able to remove the clouds of fear.

———◆———

And you will hear of wars and rumors of wars; **see that you are not frightened** or troubled, for this must take place, but the end is not yet.

Matthew 24:6 (AMP)

When our hearts are fixed and trusting in God we are able to be at peace and unafraid of outside troubles that we have no control over.

The angel said to the women, "**Do not be afraid**; for I know that you are looking for Jesus who has been crucified. He is not here, for He has risen, just as He said. Come, see the place where He was lying."

Matthew 28:5-6 (NASB)

Do not allow fear to mislead or fool you with things that are not true. We have no cause to be afraid when we place our faith in God's promises because they are true. Seek Him and you will find Him, and then look forward to meeting Him face to face. He is our reward.

———————◆———————

Then Jesus said to them, "**Do not be afraid**. Go and tell my brothers to go to Galilee; there they will see me."

Matthew 28:10 (NIV)

Christ is risen, He is with us. His resurrection silences fear and fills us with hope and joy. Now go out and proclaim it!

Jesus got up and ordered the wind and the waves to be quiet. The wind stopped, and everything was calm. Jesus asked his disciples, **"Why were you afraid? Don't you have any faith?"** Now they were more afraid than ever and said to each other, "Who is this? Even the wind and the waves obey him!"

Mark 4:39-41 (CEV)

When we have faith in ALL matters our fears turn to calm. Give honor and praise to God who is gracious and all powerful.

———◆———

While Jesus was still speaking, some people came from the house of the synagogue leader. They said, "Your daughter is dead. There is no need to bother the teacher anymore." But Jesus paid no attention to what they said. He told the synagogue leader, **"Don't be afraid**; just believe."

Mark 5:35-36 (NCV)

The treatment for anguish and fear is faith. We rest on the promises of Christ and depend on Him to do what is right.

But when they saw Him walking on the sea, they supposed that it was a ghost, and cried out; for they all saw Him and were terrified. But immediately He spoke with them and said to them, "Take courage; it is I, **do not be afraid**." Then He got into the boat with them, and the wind stopped; and they were utterly astonished,

Mark 6:49-51 (NASB)

Cry out to Christ when darkness and clouds are present. His comforting voice and presence are enough to provide courage and calm the storm.

———————◆———————

They came to him and said, "Teacher, we know that you are an honest man. **You are not afraid** of what other people think about you, because you pay no attention to who they are. And you teach the truth about God's way. Tell us: Is it right to pay taxes to Caesar or not?

Mark 12:14 (NCV)

Though others may take issue or be offended, we will boldly speak God's truth and give our adoration and ourselves to Him.

And when you hear of wars and rumors of wars, **do not get alarmed (troubled and frightened)**; it is necessary [that these things] take place, but the end is not yet.

Mark 13:7 (AMP)

When it seems like your world is crumbling around you, take comfort in knowing you possess heavenly security.

————◆————

He said, "**Don't be afraid**. I know you're looking for Jesus the Nazarene, the One they nailed on the cross. He's been raised up; he's here no longer. You can see for yourselves that the place is empty. Now—on your way. Tell his disciples and Peter that he is going on ahead of you to Galilee. You'll see him there, exactly as he said."

Mark 16:6-7 (MSG)

Do not dwell on sorrowful times or things of the past, but rejoice and believe in what is ahead. Remember that Christ goes before us to prepare a way.

But the angel said to him: "**Do not be afraid**, Zechariah; your prayer has been heard. Your wife Elizabeth will bear you a son, and you are to give him the name John."

Luke 1:13 (NIV)

We are comforted in knowing that our prayers are always heard.

————◆————

The angel came to her and said, "Greetings! The Lord has blessed you and is with you." But Mary was very startled by what the angel said and wondered what this greeting might mean. The angel said to her, "**Don't be afraid**, Mary; God has shown you his grace."

Luke 1:28-30 (NCV)

No matter who is against us, God is for us, His grace is a special gift that we don't deserve. Do not surrender to unbelieving fear.

We have been rescued from our enemies so we can serve God **without fear**, in holiness and righteousness for as long as we live.

Luke 1:74-75 (NLT)

By God's grace we are commissioned to serve Him with a fearless spirit of obedience and a confident attitude knowing, that we are secure from the fear of evil.

———◆———

And, lo, the angel of the Lord came upon them, and the glory of the Lord shone round about them: and they were sore afraid. And the angel said unto them, **Fear not**: for, behold, I bring you good tidings of great joy, which shall be to all people.

Luke 2:9-10 (KJV)

Our fears turn to joy when we embrace the good news.

But when Simon Peter saw it, he fell down at Jesus' knees, saying, "Depart from me, for I am a sinful man, O Lord." For he and all who were with him were astonished at the catch of fish that they had taken, and so also were James and John, sons of Zebedee, who were partners with Simon. And Jesus said to Simon, **"Do not be afraid**; from now on you will be catching men." And when they had brought their boats to land, they left everything and followed him.

Luke 5:8-11 (ESV)

What greater things does Christ have in store for us, put the fears and cares of this world behind you and boldly follow Him.

———————◆———————

While He was still speaking, someone came from the house of the synagogue official, saying, "Your daughter has died; do not trouble the Teacher anymore." But when Jesus heard this, He answered him, **"Do not be afraid** any longer; only believe, and she will be made well."

Luke 8:49-50 (NASB)

Be bold and passionate in your faith in Christ, depend on His doing great things, even beyond what you are able to imagine.

I tell you, my friends, **do not be afraid** of those who kill the body and after that can do no more. But I will show you whom you should fear: Fear him who, after the killing of the body, has power to throw you into hell. Yes, I tell you, fear him.

Luke 12:4-5 (NIV)

We have a friend in Jesus, so be bold in your faith walk and worship the One who is all powerful and in control, those who have a holy fear of God need not fear any man.

———————◆———————

Are not five sparrows sold for two farthings, and not one of them is forgotten before God? But even the very hairs of your head are all numbered. **Fear not** therefore: ye are of more value than many sparrows.

Luke 12:6-7 (KJV)

Place your confidence in the Father who provides comfort. Be encouraged because He is aware of even the smallest details. We are valuable in His sight.

So **don't be afraid**, little flock. For it gives your Father great happiness to give you the Kingdom.

Luke 12:32 (NLT)

We have a hope in a kingdom that overcomes the fears of this world, and a good Shepherd that protects us.

———◆———

Jesus replied: Don't be fooled by those who will come and claim to be me. They will say, "I am Christ!" and "Now is the time!" But don't follow them. When you hear about wars and riots, **don't be afraid**. These things will have to happen first, but that isn't the end.

Luke 21:8-9 (CEV)

We trust in the gospel message and look beyond visible trials for which fear has no power to affect. Live in a way that you are always ready.

While Jesus' disciples were talking about what had happened, Jesus appeared and greeted them. They were frightened and terrified because they thought they were seeing a ghost. But Jesus said, **"Why are you so frightened?** Why do you doubt? Look at my hands and my feet and see who I am! Touch me and find out for yourselves. Ghosts don't have flesh and bones as you see I have."

Luke 24:36-39 (CEV)

Fear and grief rise from our own troublesome thoughts, but the peace of Christ is able to lay them to rest.

———————◆———————

Meanwhile, the sea was getting rough and rising high because of a great and violent wind that was blowing. [However] when they had rowed three or four miles, they saw Jesus walking on the sea and approaching the boat. And they were afraid (terrified). But Jesus said to them, It is I; **be not afraid!** [I AM; **stop being frightened!**] Then they were quite willing and glad for Him to come into the boat. And now the boat went at once to the land they had steered toward. [And immediately they reached the shore toward which they had been slowly making their way.]

John 6:18-21 (AMP)

When the storms of fear erupt, Christ is there to provide reassurance and safe passage from it.

"**Don't be afraid**, people of Jerusalem. Look, your King is coming, riding on a donkey's colt."

John 12:15 (NLT)

Do not allow fear to rob you from spiritual joy. Rejoice; Christ comes to silence fear.

———————◆———————

Peace I leave with you; My [own] peace I now give and bequeath to you. Not as the world gives do I give to you. **Do not let your hearts** be troubled, neither let them **be afraid**. [Stop allowing yourselves to be agitated and disturbed; and **do not permit yourselves to be fearful** and intimidated and cowardly and unsettled.]

John 14:27 (AMP)

Do not give in to fear and dwell on what might have been or what may occur. The peace of Christ provides victory over fear.

What David said are really the words of Jesus, "I always see the Lord near me, and I **will not be afraid** with him at my right side. Because of this, my heart will be glad, my words will be joyful, and I will live in hope."

Acts 2:25-26 (CEV)

Look to the confidence of Christ during hardship knowing, like Jesus, that the Father strengthens and guides and that a glorious end will be the Lord's pleasure.

———————◆———————

When he came to Jerusalem, he tried to join the disciples, but **they were all afraid of him**, not believing that he really was a disciple. **But Barnabas** took him and **brought him to the apostles.** He told them how Saul on his journey had seen the Lord and that the Lord had spoken to him, and how in Damascus he had preached fearlessly in the name of Jesus. So Saul stayed with them and moved about freely in Jerusalem, speaking boldly in the name of the Lord.

Acts 9:26-28 (TNIV)

A trusting friend can help dismiss unfounded fear, how wonderful it is that we have a friend in Jesus.

FEARFUL TO FEARLESS

One night the Lord spoke to Paul in a vision and told him, "**Don't be afraid!** Speak out! Don't be silent! For I am with you, and no one will attack and harm you, for many people in this city belong to me."

Acts 18:9-10 (NLT)

Since we have Christ with us we can speak fearlessly and courageously with all the liberty of spirit that comes as an ambassador for Christ.

———◆———

That night the Lord stood by Paul and said, "**Don't be afraid**! You have given your witness for me here in Jerusalem, and you must also do the same in Rome."

Acts 23:11 (GNT)

Christ is by our side both day and night. Do not fear what might lie ahead, for it is Christ's will for us to always serve faithfully and cheerfully.

94

For last night an angel of the God to whom I belong and whom I worship came to me and said, **"Don't be afraid**, Paul! You must stand before the Emperor. And God in his goodness to you has spared the lives of all those who are sailing with you."

Acts 27:23-24 (GNT)

Do not fear the storms of life, and take satisfaction when others are blessed as a result of God's blessing upon you.

————◆————

For **the Spirit that God** has given you **does not** make you slaves and **cause you to be afraid**; instead, the Spirit makes you God's children, and by the Spirit's power we cry out to God, "Father! my Father!" God's Spirit joins himself to our spirits to declare that we are God's children.

Romans 8:15-16 (GNT)

As followers of Christ we are privileged to enjoy a spirit of adoption with the Father, not a spirit of fear. We come to the Father through prayer and dependence as His children.

Isaiah **was fearless** enough to tell that the Lord had said, "I was found by people who were not looking for me. I appeared to the ones who were not asking about me."

Romans 10:20 (CEV)

We give thanks to God for choosing us in love and can be bold and fearless when speaking His truth. Do not be afraid of upsetting men.

———————◆———————

THEREFORE, SINCE we do hold and engage in this ministry by the mercy of God [granting us favor, benefits, opportunities, and especially salvation], **we do not get** discouraged (spiritless and **despondent with fear**) or become faint with weariness and exhaustion. We have renounced disgraceful ways (secret thoughts, feelings, desires and underhandedness, the methods and arts that men hide through shame); we refuse to deal craftily (to practice trickery and cunning) or to adulterate or handle dishonestly the Word of God, but we state the truth openly (clearly and candidly). And so we commend ourselves in the sight and presence of God to every man's conscience.

2 Corinthians 4:1-2 (AMP)

Through Gods grace and mercy He counts us as faithful. This same grace and mercy allows us to serve Him honestly and in all sincerity, thereby bringing Him glory.

Therefore **we do not become** discouraged (utterly spiritless, exhausted, and **wearied out through fear**). Though our outer man is [progressively] decaying and wasting away, yet our inner self is being [progressively] renewed day after day.

2 Corinthians 4:16 (AMP)

If adversity and hardship contribute to the renewal of our soul then we will be glad and not afraid. Be continually renewed each day through His word.

———————◆———————

That was God's plan from the beginning. He has worked it out through Christ Jesus our Lord. Through him and through faith in him we can approach God. We can come to him freely. We can **come without fear**.

Ephesians 3:11-12 (NIrV)

We have no obstacles to God because of our faith in Christ. We can go to Him in confidence and not be afraid.

Pray also for me, that whenever I speak, words may be given me so that I will **fearlessly make known** the mystery of the gospel, for which I am an ambassador in chains. Pray that I may **declare it fearlessly**, as I should.

Ephesians 6:19-20 (TNIV)

We declare victory over fear through heavenly petition for courage and boldness.

So **don't be afraid** in any way of those who oppose you. That will show them that they will be destroyed and that you will be saved. That's what God will do.

Philippians 1:28 (NIrV)

When we stand up to intimidation from the enemy we encourage others and confirm our faith in the gospel of Christ.

Do not become easily upset in your thinking or **afraid** if you hear that the day of the Lord has already come. Someone may have said this in a prophecy or in a message or in a letter as if it came from us.

2 Thessalonians 2:2 (NCV)

Fear and deception can cripple faith. Pray and always be watchful so we do not waiver in the truth.

For God hath **not given us the spirit of fear;** but of power, and of love, and of a sound mind.

2 Timothy 1:7 (KJV)

Fear is a hindrance to the usefulness of our gifts. The spirit of power overcomes difficulties, the spirit of love for God carries us through opposition and hurt, and the spirit of sound mind overcomes our own discouragement.

———◆———

Because God's children are human beings—made of flesh and blood—the Son also became flesh and blood. For only as a human being could he die, and only by dying could he break the power of the devil, who had the power of death. Only in this way could **he set free** all who have lived their lives as slaves to **the fear of dying**.

Hebrews 2:14-15 (NLT)

Christ came to defeat death so that our souls would be at peace knowing that we will not be separated from the love of God. What once belonged to the devil is now owned by Christ and is our pathway to eternal life.

Let us then **fearlessly** and confidently and boldly **draw near** to the throne of grace (the throne of God's unmerited favor to us sinners), that we may receive mercy [for our failures] and find grace to help in good time for every need [appropriate help and well-timed help, coming just when we need it].

Hebrews 4:16 (AMP)

We are dependent on God for each day. Take comfort in His invitation for us to lay our prayers before Him in faith and confidence, whether during periods of prosperity or adversity, assuredness or confusion, bravery or fearfulness.

———◆———

Do not, therefore, fling away your **fearless confidence**, for it carries a great and glorious compensation of reward.

Hebrews 10:35 (AMP)

Never abandon your confident trust in the Lord; remain bold and courageous in your faith, for a great reward awaits you.

Moses' parents had faith. So they hid him for three months after he was born. They saw he was a special child. They **were not afraid** of the king's command.

Hebrews 11:23 (NIrV)

Our faith is a safeguard against the sinful fear of men.

———◆———

He reckoned that to suffer scorn for the Messiah was worth far more than all the treasures of Egypt, for he kept his eyes on the future reward. It was faith that made Moses leave Egypt **without being afraid** of the king's anger. As though he saw the invisible God, he refused to turn back.

Hebrews 11:26-27 (GNT)

Through faith we are assured of the Father's presence and able to look beyond fear to our heavenly reward.

Keep your lives free from the love of money, and be satisfied with what you have. For God has said, "I will never leave you; I will never abandon you." Let us be bold, then, and say, "The Lord is my helper, I will **not be afraid**. What can anyone do to me?"

Hebrews 13:5-6 (GNT)

With God as our helper, we have no need to fear, envy or be dissatisfied. He will never leave nor turn His back on us, so be content with what God has blessed you with.

———◆———

but let it be the hidden person of the heart, with the imperishable quality of a gentle and quiet spirit, which is precious in the sight of God. For in this way in former times the holy women also, who hoped in God, used to adorn themselves, being submissive to their own husbands; just as Sarah obeyed Abraham, calling him lord, and you have become her children if you do what is right **without being frightened by any fear**.

1 Peter 3:4-6 (NASB)

Be committed to one another, not out of fear or by force, but from a willing heart, and in obedience to the command of God, from a desire to do well and to please Him.

Who is going to harm you if you are eager to do good? But even if you should suffer for what is right, you are blessed. **"Do not fear what they fear; do not be frightened."** But in your hearts set apart Christ as Lord. Always be prepared to give an answer to everyone who asks you to give the reason for the hope that you have.

1 Peter 3:13-15a (NIV)

Do not be afraid of your enemies. Your enemies are God's enemies, and they can do nothing to you unless allowed by His permission. Instead sanctify the Lord in your hearts through sincere reverence, trusting his faithfulness, submitting to His wisdom and giving Him glory.

◆

Whoever confesses that Jesus is the Son of God has God living inside, and that person lives in God. And so we know the love that God has for us, and we trust that love. God is love. Those who live in love live in God, and God lives in them. This is how love is made perfect in us: that **we can be without fear** on the day God judges us, because in this world we are like him.

1 John 4:15-17 (NCV)

God showed His love through Christ whom we declare as our Savior. Through our trust and adoration in Him, love abounds...where love abounds, there is no fear.

103

Where God's love is, there is **no fear**, because God's **perfect love drives out fear**. It is punishment that makes a person fear, so love is not made perfect in the person who fears.

1 John 4:18 (NCV)

Those who dread God's punishment are afraid of Him because of their sin. Believers fear God in worshipful ways, giving Him honor and praise for His authority and love for us. This love eliminates any cause for being afraid.

———————◆———————

When I saw him, I fell down at his feet like a dead man. He placed his right hand on me and said, "**Don't be afraid!** I am the first and the last."

Revelation 1:17 (GNT)

God is all powerful, yet speaks to us personally. He reaches out to comfort, encourage and strengthen us.

Do not be afraid of what you are about to suffer. I tell you, the devil will put some of you in prison to test you, and you will suffer persecution for ten days. Be faithful, even to the point of death, and I will give you the crown of life.

Revelation 2:10 (NIV)

Trials are the works of the devils influence on wicked men. But we are not afraid because we have been armed with the knowledge of eternity and know that our trials are only temporary.

Do Not Worry

do not be anxious about anything, but in everything by prayer and supplication with thanksgiving let your requests be made known to God. And the peace of God, which surpasses all understanding, will guard your hearts and your minds in Christ Jesus.

Philippians 4:6-7 (ESV)

Today is the tomorrow you worried about yesterday.

~ Author Unknown

Everyone experiences anxiety at times; it's a normal part of life that can help in solving problems and serves to warn us in dangerous situations. External factors including school and work, relationships and finances and even medical conditions can all contribute to feeling anxious.

The problem is when anxiety and worry consumes us, when we are filled with negative questions and forever dwell on "what if" situations that can suck the energy right out of us. It's down right unhealthy and can be the cause of frequent mood swings and even destroy relationships. Sometimes it reaches the point where counseling or medical treatments are required.

Anxiety in a man's heart weighs him down,
but a good word makes him glad.

Proverbs 12:25 (ESV)

The word of God teaches that we are to turn to Him and His words, and in turn He will replace our trouble and worry with joy.

I am filled with trouble and anxiety, but your
commandments bring me joy.

Psalm 119:143 (GNT)

I'm reminded of an old fable that goes by many names, 'Chicken Little', 'Chicken Licken' and 'Henny Penny' to name a few.

The story begins with Chicken Licken convinced that the sky is falling when an acorn falls on her head. On her way to notify the king she persuades all the other animals she encounters along the way that the sky is indeed falling. She says that she saw it with her own eyes, heard it with her own ears, and even felt it when a piece hit her on the head. All the animals join her on her quest when they ultimately meet up with Foxy Loxy who comes up with a diabolical plan to trick them by telling them of a short cut which ultimately leads to Foxy Loxy's den.

The story has many different endings, but in the story I remember the animals are ultimately confronted by the 'Wise Old Owl' who exposes Foxy Loxy's fiendish plans and they all escape safely.

All the worry, all the excitement, all the hysteria caused by believing everything you hear and jumping to conclusions, when in the end a little wisdom, a little enlightenment, a bit of prudence and good judgment was all that was necessary to be able to discern the truth.

If any of you lacks wisdom, he should ask God, who gives generously to all without finding fault, and it will be given to him.

James 1:5 (NIV)

God is able to use all things for His good, so put your hope in Him, give Him thanks and hand over to Him all your troubles and all your worries, and allow His peace to comfort you.

Join me as we explore God's compassionate and comforting words on worry and anxiety to be encouraged in becoming more bold, courageous, trusting and faithful each day.

But God said to Abraham, **Don't be worried** about the boy and your slave Hagar. Do whatever Sarah tells you, because it is through Isaac that you will have the descendants I have promised. I will also give many children to the son of the slave woman, so that they will become a nation. He too is your son.

Genesis 21:12-13 (GNT)

When we are clear in knowing what God expects of us, we are better able to make difficult choices without worry.

———◆———

The servant said, **Don't worry**. Don't be afraid. Your God, the God of your father, must have put the money in your sacks for you. I received your payment. Then he brought Simeon to them.

Genesis 43:23 (GNT)

We are indebted to God for all of our happiness and blessings and for the compassion and generosity of our friends. Do not worry or ask how or why; accept it as divine guidance.

He said to his brothers, "I am Joseph. Is my father still alive?" But the brothers could not answer him, because they were very afraid of him. So Joseph said to them, "Come close to me." When the brothers came close to him, he said to them, "I am your brother Joseph, whom you sold as a slave to go to Egypt. Now **don't be worried** or angry with yourselves because you sold me here. God sent me here ahead of you to save people's lives."

Genesis 45:3-5 (NCV)

What a comfort it is that Christ is close by to reassure us when we are afraid and to forgive when we are filled with remorse. Our Father is all powerful and able to use all things for His good.

———————◆———————

Then Pharaoh said to Joseph, "Tell your brothers, 'Take wagons from the land of Egypt to carry your little children and your wives, and bring your father here. **Don't worry** about your personal belongings, for the best of all the land of Egypt is yours.'"

Genesis 45:19-20 (NLT)

Do not worry or set your eyes or heart upon the stuff of this world, there is a heavenly glory set aside for us through Christ.

If you obey my laws and teachings, you will live safely in the land and enjoy its abundant crops. **Don't ever worry** about what you will eat during the seventh year when you are forbidden to plant or harvest. I will see to it that you harvest enough in the sixth year to last for three years.

Leviticus 25:18-21 (CEV)

When we cast our cares on the Father we demonstrate trust and reliance on Him and have assurance of His protection and blessed provision.

———————◆———————

They said to him, "Please ask God if we are going to be successful on our trip." The priest answered, "**You have nothing to worry about**. The Lord is taking care of you on this trip."

Judges 18:5-6 (GNT)

Be on the same path that is acceptable to God and take comfort in knowing that He goes before us.

Naomi replied, "Just be patient and **don't worry** about what will happen. He won't rest until everything is settled today!"

Ruth 3:18 (CEV)

When we turn our concerns over to God we are assured that He will work them for His good.

———————◆———————

"Sir, please don't think I'm no good!" Hannah answered. "I'm not drunk, and I haven't been drinking. But I do feel miserable and terribly upset. I've been praying all this time, telling the LORD about my problems." Eli replied, "You may go home now and **stop worrying**. I'm sure the God of Israel will answer your prayer."

1 Samuel 1:15-17 (CEV)

Earnest prayer is a comfort to our soul; we trust that when we leave our worries with Him, He will answer in a way that is most fitting for us.

Samuel answered, "I am the seer. Go with me to the place of worship. Today you and your servant are to eat with me. Tomorrow morning I will answer all your questions and send you home. **Don't worry** about the donkeys you lost three days ago, because they have been found. Soon all the wealth of Israel will belong to you and your family."

1 Samuel 9:19-20 (NCV)

If a prophet can provide answers to questions that have yet to be asked, how much more can God understand your thoughts and deepest worries?

———◆———

The LORD sent Gideon, Bedan, Jephthah, and Samuel to rescue you from your enemies, and **you didn't have to worry** about being attacked.

1 Samuel 12:11 (CEV)

Hold strong to your faith in God; be encouraged by reminding yourself of previous blessings and victories over fear and worry.

Be kind to me. After all, it was your idea to promise the LORD that we would always be loyal friends. If I've done anything wrong, kill me yourself, but don't hand me over to your father. "**Don't worry**," Jonathan said. "If I find out that my father wants to kill you, I'll certainly let you know."

1 Samuel 20:8-9 (CEV)

The reassurance from a loyal friend is comforting and able to calm our worry, the love and comfort from the Lord endures forever, He never waivers.

———◆———

The Levites encouraged the people by saying, "This is a sacred day, so **don't worry** or mourn!"

Nehemiah 8:11 (CEV)

We rejoice in the understanding of God's word. It is an encouragement to us that provides both conviction and comfort.

You will rest safe and secure, filled with hope and **emptied of worry**. You will sleep without fear and be greatly respected.

Job 11:18-19 (CEV)

Hope is a pillar of the soul. Those with hope in God, through grace, have no reason to worry or be afraid.

———◆———

I look to the Lord for help at all times, and he rescues me from danger. Turn to me, Lord, and be merciful to me, because I am lonely and weak. **Relieve me of my worries** and save me from all my troubles. Consider my distress and suffering and forgive all my sins.

Psalm 25:15-18 (GNT)

When we are filled with worry we can look to the Lord for mercy. He is the one who can forgive and save.

Don't be worried on account of the wicked; don't be jealous of those who do wrong. They will soon disappear like grass that dries up; they will die like plants that wither.

Psalm 37:1-2 (GNT)

Having a spirit of content and confidence in God is sufficient to keep us from being envious of the success and prosperity of men which is short lived. With God our future is everlasting.

———◆———

Be patient and wait for the Lord to act; **don't be worried** about those who prosper or those who succeed in their evil plans.

Psalm 37:7 (GNT)

We wait expectantly for the Lord and put aside any worry, because we know that all that He does, and all He allows, He is able to use for His good.

Don't give in to worry or anger; it only leads to trouble. Those who trust in the Lord will possess the land, but the wicked will be driven out.

Psalm 37:8-9 (GNT)

When we give in to anger and worry over the prosperity of those who do evil we open ourselves up to temptation. The actions of the wicked are costly and judgment is certain.

———◆———

I kept quiet, not saying a word, not even about anything good! But my suffering only grew worse, and I was **overcome with anxiety**. The more I thought, the more troubled I became;

Psalm 39:2-3a (GNT)

Speculation and worry only serve to feed discontent. Through prayer we seek forgiveness and wisdom to counteract dissatisfaction and discontentment.

———◆———

Our God says, "**Calm down**, and learn that I am God! All nations on earth will honor me."

Psalm 46:10 (CEV)

Be still and do not worry, for God is God and rules the nations, His name will be exalted.

Hear my prayer, O God; don't turn away from my plea! Listen to me and answer me; I am **worn out by my worries**. I am terrified by the threats of my enemies, crushed by the oppression of the wicked. They bring trouble on me; they are angry with me and hate me.

Psalm 55:1-3 (GNT)

Confidence in your own strength can give way to fear and worry, but prayerfully laying open your heart to God and placing confidence in Him gives hope of His protection.

Turn your worries over to the Lord. He will keep you going. He will never let godly people fall.

Psalm 55:22 (NIrV)

God in His own way and in His own timing is able to quiet our worries. Through prayer and faith we entrust them to His care.

When **my anxious thoughts multiply within me**, Your consolations delight my soul.

Psalm 94:19 (NASB)

When anxious thoughts swirl in our heads God is able to bring relief to our soul, timely relief that brings a calming peace that worldly comforts cannot.

He is **not worried** or afraid; he is certain to see his enemies defeated.

Psalm 112:8 (GNT)

Even though we may experience troubles and adversity we will not be anxious, for we know that the Lord is able to deliver us and that our spiritual enemies are destined for defeat.

————◆————

I love the Lord, because he hears me; he listens to my prayers. He listens to me every time I call to him. The danger of death was all around me; the horrors of the grave closed in on me; **I was filled with fear and anxiety**. Then I called to the Lord, I beg you, Lord, save me!

Psalm 116:1-4 (GNT)

When it seems like you are at the end of your rope, do not allow fear and anxiousness to get the best of you as it only serves to compound issues. God loves to hear from us, so turn to Him in faithful prayer and place yourself under His protection, let prayer be your first resort... not your last.

You are kind, LORD, so good and merciful. You protect ordinary people, and when I was helpless, you saved me and treated me so kindly that **I don't need to worry** anymore. You, LORD, have saved my life from death, my eyes from tears, my feet from stumbling. Now I will walk at your side in this land of the living.

Psalm 116:5-9 (CEV)

In faith we place ourselves in the safety and protection of our Father. We commit ourselves to walk by His side without fear or worry for He has rescued our soul from death.

———◆———

When I was really hurting, I prayed to the LORD. He answered my prayer, and **took my worries away**.

Psalm 118:5 (CEV)

When we humble ourselves to God in prayer he is able to quiet our worry in ways we cannot even perceive.

I am **filled with trouble and anxiety**, but your commandments bring me joy.

Psalm 119:143 (GNT)

In the midst of our trouble and worry we are comforted by the word of God. Desire wisdom and understanding of His word to be revealed.

———◆———

Search me, O God, and know my heart; test me and **know my anxious thoughts**.

Psalm 139:23 (NLT)

Let God search and expose the fear in us so that we may be cleansed of it, for our desire is to be free from fear and anxiety in order to be pleasing to Him.

———◆———

Anxiety in a man's heart weighs him down, but a good word makes him glad.

Proverbs 12:25 (ESV)

Anxiousness and fear are disabling to our heart and spirit. The prescription is a good word from God, obtained through prayer and put to use in faith.

Don't let evil people worry you; don't be envious of them. A wicked person has no future—nothing to look forward to.

Proverbs 24:19-20 (GNT)

The success of those that are corrupt is short lived because it only exists for this present life. Do not be envious or concern yourself with it for your reward is in heaven.

---◆---

She doesn't worry when it snows, because her family has warm clothing.

Proverbs 31:21 (GNT)

When we are equipped with the word of God we are effectively prepared to face the chill of fear during life's storms.

You work and **worry your way through life**, and what do you have to show for it? As long as you live, everything you do brings **nothing but worry** and heartache. Even at night your mind can't rest. It is all useless.

Ecclesiastes 2:22-23 (GNT)

Those that are prone to anxiousness discover that the more worldly they are, the more anxious they become. Make God your refuge both day and night, and be thankful for everything that comes from Him.

———◆———

God gives some people the ability to enjoy the wealth and property he gives them, as well as the ability to accept their state in life and enjoy their work. They **do not worry** about how short life is, because God keeps them busy with what they love to do.

Ecclesiastes 5:19-20 (NCV)

Be glad and generous with what God has given. Take pleasure in the work you have been called to. Having a cheerful heart and attitude is a great blessing and eases our burdens.

I tried to understand all that happens on earth. I saw how busy people are, working day and night and hardly ever sleeping. I also saw all that God has done. Nobody can understand what God does here on earth. **No matter how hard people try to understand it, they cannot**. Even if wise people say they understand, they cannot; no one can really understand it.

Ecclesiastes 8:16-17 (NCV)

Do not worry about what happens in this world or even what God is up to. His ways are above our ways, and He is able to use all things for His good.

————◆————

If you worry about the weather and don't plant seeds, you won't harvest a crop.

Ecclesiastes 11:4 (CEV)

Do not get bogged down and worry over the little things in life. If we wait for conditions to be perfect before sowing seed we will never reap the fruit.

Don't let anything worry you or cause you pain. You aren't going to be young very long.

Ecclesiastes 11:10 (GNT)

The pleasures and desires of the world will all pass away. Live your life in a way that is pleasing to God because it is good for both the body and the soul, and alleviates our worry as we look back on our short lives.

———◆———

Tell Ahaz, 'Be careful. **Be calm and don't worry.** Don't let those two men, Rezin and Pekah son of Remaliah, scare you. Don't be afraid of their anger or Aram's anger, because they are like two barely burning sticks that are ready to go out. They have made plans against you, saying, "Let's fight against Judah and tear it apart. We will divide the land for ourselves and make the son of Tabeel the new king of Judah." But I, the Lord God, say, "Their plan will not succeed; it will not happen,"'

Isaiah 7:4-7 (NCV)

Do not let the anger of those that are against God cause you to be afraid or worry, their threats are ultimately snuffed out. God is our consuming fire that is able to extinguish fear and worry.

God's people will be **free from worries**, and their homes peaceful and safe.

Isaiah 32:18 (GNT)

The righteousness of God that dwells within us is sufficient to deliver us from worry.

[Most] blessed is the man who believes in, trusts in, and relies on the Lord, and whose hope and confidence the Lord is. For he shall be like a tree planted by the waters that spreads out its roots by the river; and it shall not see and fear when heat comes; but its leaf shall be green. It shall **not be anxious and full of care** in the year of drought, nor shall it cease yielding fruit.

Jeremiah 17:7-8 (AMP)

God is our hope, we trust in His power and strength to carry us during times of drought. We will not worry or be afraid for He is our fountain providing us with inward peace and satisfaction.

Therefore I tell you, **do not be anxious** about your life, what you will eat or what you will drink, nor about your body, what you will put on. Is not life more than food, and the body more than clothing? Look at the birds of the air: they neither sow nor reap nor gather into barns, and yet your heavenly Father feeds them. Are you not of more value than they?

Matthew 6:25-26 (ESV)

God is able to provide for all our needs and guard against evil. If we choose to trust in Him instead of worrying about things of the world it is better for our souls.

———◆———

And **who of you by worrying and being anxious** can add one unit of measure (cubit) to his stature or to the span of his life?

Matthew 6:27 (AMP)

God made us as He designed, do not be anxious about life, but be content and trust in Him to provide for your needs.

And **why do you worry** about clothes? Look at how the lilies in the field grow. They don't work or make clothes for themselves. But I tell you that even Solomon with his riches was not dressed as beautifully as one of these flowers. God clothes the grass in the field, which is alive today but tomorrow is thrown into the fire. So you can be even more sure that God will clothe you. Don't have so little faith!

Matthew 6:28-30 (NCV)

Cast your cares on God, trust in Him who is able to provide all things, for things of this world fade and wither away.

———————◆———————

Don't worry and say, 'What will we eat?' or 'What will we drink?' or 'What will we wear?' The people who don't know God keep trying to get these things, and your Father in heaven knows you need them. Seek first God's kingdom and what God wants. Then all your other needs will be met as well.

Matthew 6:31-33 (NCV)

Our Father knows our needs and is able to supply all, so trust in His wisdom and power to provide, and leave it to the unbeliever to be anxious about worldly things, for they do not know God.

Give your entire attention to what God is doing right now, and **don't get worked up** about what may or may not happen tomorrow. God will help you deal with whatever hard things come up when the time comes.

Matthew 6:34 (MSG)

It serves no purpose to be preoccupied with what might happen, so don't worry about tomorrow; let God be God in your life today.

————◆————

Some people soon brought to him a crippled man lying on a mat. When Jesus saw how much faith they had, he said to the crippled man, "My friend, **don't worry**! Your sins are forgiven."

Matthew 9:2 (CEV)

Regardless of our difficulties we can be free from worry and criticism. We rejoice in Christ and the forgiveness of sin.

————◆————

Jesus turned. He saw the woman and said, "**Don't worry**! You are now well because of your faith." At that moment she was healed.

Matthew 9:22 (CEV)

When we approach Christ in faith and love, with a firm hope in the promise, Christ is able to comfort us through even our most private fears.

131

Don't be naive. Some people will impugn your motives, others will smear your reputation—just because you believe in me. Don't be upset when they haul you before the civil authorities. Without knowing it, they've done you—and me—a favor, given you a platform for preaching the kingdom news! And **don't worry** about what you'll say or how you'll say it. The right words will be there; the Spirit of your Father will supply the words.

Matthew 10:17-20 (MSG)

Like sheep among the wolves we are sent by Christ, though we are free of worry because we place our reliance on God rather than our own abilities. When we speak for Him we trust in His Spirit of wisdom.

———————◆———————

Others received the seed that fell among the thorns. They are those who hear the message. But then the **worries of this life** and the false promises of wealth crowd it out. They keep it from producing fruit.

Matthew 13:22 (NIrV)

Worrying over things of the world is a distraction to the word of God. Put your confidence in Him rather than worldly treasures.

The seed that fell among the thorns represents others who hear God's word, but all too quickly the message is crowded out by the **worries of this life**, the lure of wealth, and the desire for other things, so no fruit is produced.

Mark 4:18-19 (NLT)

Do not be concerned with the pleasures and desires of the world; they are an obstruction to our being deeply rooted in the Word of God.

———————◆———————

While Jesus was still speaking, some men came from Jairus' home and said, "Your daughter has died! Why bother the teacher anymore?" Jesus heard what they said, and he said to Jairus, "**Don't worry**. Just have faith!"

Mark 5:35-36 (CEV)

The treatment for anguish and fear is faith. We rest on the promises of Christ and depend on Him to do what is right.

They came to him and said, "Teacher, we know that you tell the truth, **without worrying** about what people think. You pay no attention to anyone's status, but teach the truth about God's will for people. Tell us, is it against our Law to pay taxes to the Roman Emperor? Should we pay them or not?"

Mark 12:14 (GNT)

Though others may take issue or be offended, we will boldly speak God's truth and give our adoration and ourselves to Him.

————◆————

For the Good News must first be preached to all nations. But when you are arrested and stand trial, **don't worry** in advance about what to say. Just say what God tells you at that time, for it is not you who will be speaking, but the Holy Spirit.

Mark 13:10-11 (NLT)

As a follower of Christ we have access to divine guidance, so that in serving Him we can count on the care and wisdom of the Holy Spirit to guide us.

When his parents saw him, they were amazed. His mother said to him, "Son, why have you treated us like this? Your father and I **have been worried** about you. We have been looking for you everywhere." "Why were you looking for me?" he asked. "Didn't you know I had to be in my Father's house?"

Luke 2:48-49 (NIrV)

Seek the peace of Christ to quiet our worries and follow His example of putting the Fathers work ahead of all other business.

———◆———

The seed which fell among the thorns, these are the ones who have heard, and as they go on their way they are **choked with worries** and riches and pleasures of this life, and bring no fruit to maturity.

Luke 8:14 (NASB)

The worries and indulgences of life leave little room for fruitfulness, put them aside and resolve to bringing forth a bumper crop.

Martha **was worried** about all that had to be done. Finally, she went to Jesus and said, "Lord, doesn't it bother you that my sister has left me to do all the work by myself? Tell her to come and help me!" The Lord answered, "Martha, Martha! You are **worried and upset about so many things**, but only one thing is necessary. Mary has chosen what is best, and it will not be taken away from her."

Luke 10:40-42 (CEV)

When we are caught up and worried about the details of this life we are distracted and negligent from hearing the word of the Lord.

————◆————

"When you are brought before synagogues, rulers and authorities, **do not worry** about how you will defend yourselves or what you will say, for the Holy Spirit will teach you at that time what you should say."

Luke 12:11-12 (NIV)

During times of trial take a stand against worry and fear and choose to honor God by seeking wisdom from the Holy Spirit.

Then, turning to his disciples, Jesus said, "That is why I tell you **not to worry** about everyday life—whether you have enough food to eat or enough clothes to wear. For life is more than food, and your body more than clothing. Look at the ravens. They don't plant or harvest or store food in barns, for God feeds them. And you are far more valuable to him than any birds!"

Luke 12:22-24 (NLT)

God is the creator and caregiver of life, He knows our needs. Do not spend time in worry, but place your trust and cares upon Him.

————◆————

"And which of you **by being anxious** can add a single hour to his span of life? If then you are not able to do as small a thing as that, **why are you anxious** about the rest?"

Luke 12:25-26 (ESV)

Do not worry or complain about things beyond your control.

Consider the lilies, how they grow: they neither toil nor spin; but I tell you, not even Solomon in all his glory clothed himself like one of these. But if God so clothes the grass in the field, which is alive today and tomorrow is thrown into the furnace, how much more will He clothe you? You men of little faith! And do not seek what you will eat and what you will drink, **and do not keep worrying**. For all these things the nations of the world eagerly seek; but your Father knows that you need these things. But seek His kingdom, and these things will be added to you.

Luke 12:27-31 (NASB)

Believers are called to be dedicated in the advancement of His kingdom. Trust the Father who knows what we need and stop worrying, He will provide.

———————◆———————

"But this will be your opportunity to tell them about me. So **don't worry** in advance about how to answer the charges against you, for I will give you the right words and such wisdom that none of your opponents will be able to reply or refute you!"

Luke 21:13-15 (NLT)

Fear and worry are silenced when we honor God by seeking His wisdom and guidance.

But **don't worry**! You will be saved by being faithful to me.

Luke 21:18-19 (CEV)

Christian patience and faithfulness during suffering or difficult times safeguards our souls so that we may possess peace of mind.

———◆———

Terror will make people faint. **They will be worried** about what is happening in the world. The sun, moon and stars will be shaken from their places. "At that time people will see the Son of Man coming in a cloud. He will come with power and great glory. When these things begin to take place, stand up. Hold your head up with joy and hope. The time when you will be set free will be very close."

Luke 21:26-28 (NIrV)

Do not be angry or afraid. When the world around you appears to be falling apart, look expectantly to heaven with faith and hope for renewal.

Be careful. If you aren't, your hearts will be loaded down with wasteful living, drunkenness and the **worries of life**. Then the day the Son of Man returns will close on you like a trap. You will not be expecting it. That day will come upon every person who lives on the whole earth. Always keep watching.

Luke 21:34-36a (NIrV)

Do not indulge in or be concerned with the cares of this life, they are a distraction to your daily walk and care of your soul. Be on your constant guard.

————◆————

Do not be worried and upset, Jesus told them. Believe in God and believe also in me. There are many rooms in my Father's house, and I am going to prepare a place for you. I would not tell you this if it were not so.

John 14:1-2 (GNT)

We have joy and hope through Jesus Christ. The joy of faith is the antidote of fear and worry.

Meanwhile, as Peter was puzzling over the vision, the Holy Spirit said to him, "Three men have come looking for you. Get up, go downstairs, and go with them without hesitation. **Don't worry**, for I have sent them."

Acts 10:19-20 (NLT)

When the conviction of our call is clear we are not to worry, doubt or be fearful regardless of any previous bias we may have.

Just then three men who had been sent from Caesarea arrived at the house where we were staying. The Holy Spirit told me to go with them and **not to worry** that they were Gentiles. These six brothers here accompanied me, and we soon entered the home of the man who had sent for us. He told us how an angel had appeared to him in his home and had told him, 'Send messengers to Joppa, and summon a man named Simon Peter. He will tell you how you and everyone in your household can be saved!'

Acts 11:11-14 (NLT)

We experience intimacy with God when we are obedient and trust the promptings of the Spirit without worrying. When we fellowship with others and share and confirm experiences our faith is strengthened.

As Paul spoke on and on, a young man named Eutychus, sitting on the windowsill, became very drowsy. Finally, he fell sound asleep and dropped three stories to his death below. Paul went down, bent over him, and took him into his arms. "**Don't worry**," he said, "he's alive!" Then they all went back upstairs, shared in the Lord's Supper, and ate together. Paul continued talking to them until dawn, and then he left. Meanwhile, the young man was taken home unhurt, and everyone was greatly relieved.

Acts 20:9-12 (NLT)

Satan will stop at nothing to keep us from God. Do not be worried or alarmed at what Satan desires for evil, for God can use all things for His good.

I want you to be **free from anxieties**. The unmarried man is anxious about the things of the Lord, how to please the Lord. But the married man is anxious about worldly things, how to please his wife, and his interests are divided. And the unmarried or betrothed woman is anxious about the things of the Lord, how to be holy in body and spirit. But the married woman is anxious about worldly things, how to please her husband. I say this for your own benefit, not to lay any restraint upon you, but to promote good order and to secure your undivided devotion to the Lord.

1 Corinthians 7:32-35 (ESV)

Seek wisdom regarding your earthly responsibilities, be careful not to worry or be overly consumed with things of the world. Fewer interests in the world will allow you to place more of your attention on pleasing and worshiping God.

And we were greatly encouraged. Although we were encouraged, we felt even better when we saw how happy Titus was, because you had shown that he had **nothing to worry about**. We had told him how much we thought of you, and you did not disappoint us. Just as we have always told you the truth, so everything we told him about you has also proved to be true. Titus loves all of you very much, especially when he remembers how you obeyed him and how you trembled with fear when you welcomed him. It makes me really glad to know that I can depend on you.

2 Corinthians 7:13-16 (CEV)

Repentance, dependence and obedience result in confidence that eliminates fear and anxiety.

———————◆———————

do not be anxious about anything, but in everything by prayer and supplication with thanksgiving let your requests be made known to God. And the peace of God, which surpasses all understanding, will guard your hearts and your minds in Christ Jesus.

Philippians 4:6-7 (ESV)

Through prayer we offer up our requests and appreciation to God and seek guidance and support for all matters to show our dependency on Him. Through prayer we receive the peace and hope of God that is sufficient to calm our fears and worries.

So humble yourselves under the mighty power of God, and at the right time he will lift you up in honor. **Give all your worries and cares to God**, for he cares about you.

1 Peter 5:6-7 (NLT)

God takes notice of the good that is in His servants, to their honor and benefit. He cares for us and overlooks our many failings.

Fear God

"The fear of the LORD is the beginning of knowledge, but fools despise wisdom and discipline."

Proverbs 1:7 (NIV)

"When you fear God, you fear nothing else. When you don't fear god, you fear everything else..."

~ Oswald Chambers

A theme repeated all through the bible is the fear of God, it plays a critical role in shaping a believers life. It is a gift from God that allows us to be more receptive to the promptings of the Holy Spirit which provides for a better understanding of Him. Having a holy fear of God results in a deeper and healthier relationship with Him and guides us in our decision making.

When we are obedient to God we become more confident in Him. Just as a child matures through a combination of love and fear of her earthly father in order to walk in obedience, so too are we to love and fear the Lord so that we continue to grow and mature spiritually. As we grow our motivation for obedience is transformed from a fear of discipline to one rooted in love. When a child grows in love and respect for a parent they do not want to do anything that would disappoint them. It's the same for the believer, as we grow to love and respect the Lord, the more we should fear disappointing Him.

So as believers we are to have the "fear of God" that expresses our love for Him and results in our worshiping Him with a reverent awe that demonstrates that He is most important in our lives. But just what does that mean?

Ask yourself this question; what do you fear losing most? Do you fear losing your job, your children, or your spouse? Do you fear being alone, or for your health or for money? Whatever it is, when you follow that which you fear losing most you discover what you love most, that which is most important to you.

For where your treasure is, there your heart will be also.

Matthew 6:21 (NIV)

To fear the Lord means that losing your relationship with Him matters most to you and will have a direct impact on how you go through life making decisions.

So does it matter to you what God thinks about your relationship with Him? How do the choices you make each day, your words and actions, matter to Him? Would He be pleased with your walk? The fear of God should motivate you to be attentive in your walk.

And now, Israel, what does the LORD your God require of you? He requires only that you fear the LORD your God, and live in a way that pleases him, and love him and serve him with all your heart and soul.

Deuteronomy 10:12 (NLT)

In essence, the fear of God is to have the love of God in our lives, which is the ultimate solution to fear.

There is no fear in love. But perfect love drives out fear...

1 John 4:18 (NIV)

Join me as we explore God's compassionate and comforting words on worshiping Him.

He said, "Do not lay your hand on the boy or do anything to him, for now I know that you **fear God**, seeing you have not withheld your son, your only son, from me."

Genesis 22:12 (ESV)

When we are willing to surrender that which is most dear to us to serve our Heavenly Father we demonstrate our love and worship to Him.

———————◆———————

Because the midwives were **God-fearing**, God was good to them and gave them families of their own. And the Israelites continued to increase and become strong.

Exodus 1:20-21 (GNT)

Families are strengthened and more secure when their homes are filled with respect and reverence for God.

Moses spoke to the people: "Don't be afraid. God has come to test you and instill **a deep and reverent awe** within you so that you won't sin."

Exodus 20:20 (MSG)

Have a humble and sincere reverence of the majesty of God, be obedient to His authority and dread His displeasure. Stand in awe of Him to be motivated and attentive in your walk.

————◆————

You shall not curse the deaf, nor put a stumbling block before the blind, but shall **fear your God**: I am the LORD.

Leviticus 19:14 (NKJV)

Let the fear of God be your guide so that you may strengthen and build up your brothers and sisters rather than undermine or be bitter toward them.

————◆————

Ye shall not therefore oppress one another; but **thou shalt fear thy God**: for I am the LORD your God.

Leviticus 25:17 (KJV)

When God reigns in your life, your heart should have no desire to wrong another or take advantage for your own personal gain or vengeance.

Only give heed to yourself and keep your soul diligently, so that you do not forget the things which your eyes have seen and they do not depart from your heart all the days of your life; but make them known to your sons and your grandsons. Remember the day you stood before the LORD your God at Horeb, when the LORD said to me, 'Assemble the people to Me, that I may let them hear My words so they may **learn to fear Me** all the days they live on the earth, and that they may teach their children.'

Deuteronomy 4:9-10 (NASB)

Be in awe and worship God as you did when you first believed. Keep Him close to your heart each day so that your life will be a reflection of Him and a living demonstration of worship for others to see.

———◆———

Oh, that they had such a heart in them **that they would fear Me** and always keep all My commandments, that it might be well with them and with their children forever!

Deuteronomy 5:29 (NKJV)

Have a worshipful heart for God that is honest, sincere and willing to follow Him, not just when we are convicted of our sins or faced with tough choices, but in all circumstances.

Now this is the commandment, the statutes and the rules that the LORD your God commanded me to teach you, that you may do them in the land to which you are going over, to possess it, that you may **fear the LORD your God,** you and your son and your son's son, by keeping all his statutes and his commandments, which I command you, all the days of your life, and that your days may be long.

Deuteronomy 6:1-2 (ESV)

The fear of the Lord provides us with good conscience to follow His ways; the ways we have been taught, and the ways we are to teach.

————◆————

Thou shalt fear the LORD thy God, and serve him, and shalt swear by his name.

Deuteronomy 6:13 (KJV)

Honor and revere God; worship and serve Him in all circumstances; have confidence in Him, and pledge to trust Him and only Him.

And the LORD commanded us to do all these statutes, to **fear the LORD our God**, for our good always, that he might preserve us alive, as it is at this day.

Deuteronomy 6:24 (KJV)

God's ways are best; they are in our best interest. Worship the Lord and praise His name, we are eternally grateful for His Son in whom we are made right.

———————◆———————

And now, O Israel, what does the LORD your God ask of you but to **fear the LORD your God**, to walk in all his ways, to love him, to serve the LORD your God with all your heart and with all your soul, and to observe the LORD's commands and decrees that I am giving you today for your own good?

Deuteronomy 10:12-13 (NIV)

To fear God is to walk in His ways not ours, to love Him and desire Him for He is a great god. To devote our lives to serve Him with dedication and enthusiasm, and understand that His will for us is for our good.

155

Fear the LORD your God and serve him. Hold fast to him and take your oaths in his name.

Deuteronomy 10:20 (TNIV)

God is God, worship Him with your whole heart and soul, cling to Him and submit to His will because of His love.

————————◆————————

Assemble the people, men, women, and little ones, and the sojourner within your towns, that they may hear and **learn to fear the LORD your God**, and be careful to do all the words of this law, and that their children, who have not known it, may hear and learn to fear the LORD your God, as long as you live in the land that you are going over the Jordan to possess.

Deuteronomy 31:12-13 (ESV)

We gain wisdom through the study of His word, and worship Him through obedience to His word. May our worship be an example to those who do not know His word so that they might turn to His word.

For the LORD your God dried up the waters of the Jordan before you until you had crossed, just as the LORD your God had done to the Red Sea, which He dried up before us until we had crossed; that all the peoples of the earth may know that the hand of the LORD is mighty, so that you may **fear the LORD your God** forever.

Joshua 4:23-24 (NASB)

Remember His mercies to be encouraged to press on through whatever worries you, for God is the same today as He was yesterday. Trust in Him so that others will be encouraged to turn to Him.

———————◆———————

Now therefore **fear the LORD**, and serve him in sincerity and in truth: and put away the gods which your fathers served on the other side of the flood, and in Egypt; and serve ye the LORD.

Joshua 24:14 (KJV)

Be fully committed to the Lord, worship Him faithfully and let go of those things of the past that held you back from the truth.

Now if you **fear and worship the Lord** and listen to his voice, and if you do not rebel against the Lord's commands, then both you and your king will show that you recognize the Lord as your God. But if you rebel against the Lord's commands and refuse to listen to him, then his hand will be as heavy upon you as it was upon your ancestors.

1 Samuel 12:14-15 (NLT)

God grants his favor and protection to those who worship Him so that they may be strengthened to press on in following His ways.

————◆————

Only **fear the LORD** and serve Him in truth with all your heart; for consider what great things He has done for you.

1 Samuel 12:24 (NASB)

Let your worship be honest and straightforward, always truthful, not simply an outward exhibition. Worship and serve the Father with all your heart and reflect on what He has done for you.

The God of Israel spoke. The Rock of Israel said to me: 'The one who rules righteously, who rules in the **fear of God**, is like the light of morning at sunrise, like a morning without clouds, like the gleaming of the sun on new grass after rain.'

2 Samuel 23:3-4 (NLT)

Do not be blinded by the darkness in the world, but desire the light that rises over darkness. Christ is the light of the world that is worthy of our worship.

———————◆———————

But the LORD, who brought you up from the land of Egypt with great power and with an outstretched arm, **Him you shall fear**, and to Him you shall bow yourselves down, and to Him you shall sacrifice. The statutes and the ordinances and the law and the commandment which He wrote for you, you shall observe to do forever; and you shall not fear other gods.

2 Kings 17:36-37 (NASB)

God is all powerful and welcomes those who worship and serve Him and Him alone. Do not allow any other idol to come between you and God.

For great is the LORD, and greatly to be praised: he also is **to be feared above all gods**. For all the gods of the people are idols: but the LORD made the heavens.

1 Chronicles 16:25-26 (KJV)

Give God all glory and praise for there is none greater than He who created all things.

————◆————

And they taught in Judah, and had the book of the law of the LORD with them, and went about throughout all the cities of Judah, and taught the people. And the **fear of the LORD** fell upon all the kingdoms of the lands that were round about Judah, so that they made no war against Jehoshaphat.

2 Chronicles 17:9-10 (KJV)

Worship the Lord and allow His comfort and peace to surround you. Let His word rule in your life to direct your path.

When the surrounding kingdoms got word that God had fought Israel's enemies, the **fear of God** descended on them. Jehoshaphat heard no more from them; as long as Jehoshaphat reigned, peace reigned.

2 Chronicles 20:29-30 (MSG)

We worship God when we trust Him with our fear and worry. When He reigns in your life, others take note of the peace that only He can provide.

————◆————

What you're doing is wrong. Is there no **fear of God** left in you? Don't you care what the nations around here, our enemies, think of you?

Nehemiah 5:9 (MSG)

Do not allow the influence of the world to hinder your walk with the Lord. Worship Him and make His ways your ways, otherwise you open yourself and Christianity up to ridicule.

There was a man in the land of Uz, whose name was Job; and that man was perfect and upright, and one that **feared God**, and eschewed evil.

Job 1:1 (KJV)

Worship the Lord and allow His will to govern your life. Be ever watchful of your words and actions to protect the reputation of not only you, but more importantly of God. Turn from evil by turning to Him, and trust in Him always.

———◆———

And the LORD said to Satan, "Have you considered my servant Job, that there is none like him on the earth, a blameless and upright man, who **fears God** and turns away from evil?"

Job 1:8 (ESV)

God delights in His saints, those who love and honor Him in worship. He is our defender against the evil one who despises those that are holy and upright.

The LORD said to Satan, "Have you considered My servant Job? For there is no one like him on the earth, a blameless and upright man **fearing God** and turning away from evil. And he still holds fast his integrity, although you incited Me against him to ruin him without cause."

Job 2:3 (NASB)

God takes great pleasure when our faith is strong to provide victory over temptation. Let your faith be strengthened by each victory and give praise to Him who is worthy.

————◆————

Merely the thought of God All-Powerful makes me **tremble with fear.** God has covered me with darkness, but I refuse to be silent.

Job 23:15-17 (CEV)

Do not allow the worries of life to give you cause to lose hope, for a time is coming when a glorious light will shine through the darkness. Look to the light of God and worship Him.

And he said to man, 'Behold, the **fear of the Lord**, that is wisdom, and to turn away from evil is understanding.'

Job 28:28 (NASB)

Real wisdom only comes from God. So worship Him with all reverence and turn from evil for understanding.

————◆————

Serve the Lord with **reverent awe and worshipful fear**; rejoice and be in high spirits with trembling [lest you displease Him].

Psalm 2:11 (AMP)

God is pleased when we freely and openly worship and serve Him. We rejoice in salvation through Christ.

The statutes of the LORD are right, rejoicing the heart; The commandment of the LORD is pure, enlightening the eyes; The **fear of the LORD** is clean, enduring forever; The judgments of the LORD are true and righteous altogether. More to be desired are they than gold, Yea, than much fine gold; Sweeter also than honey and the honeycomb.

Psalm 19:8-10 (NKJV)

Be sincere and honest in your worship of the Lord and hold His laws close to your heart. The word of God is more valuable than any worldly treasure; it is the same yesterday, today and forever.

———◆———

Praise the Lord, all you who **fear him**! Honor him, all you descendants of Jacob! Show him reverence, all you descendants of Israel!

Psalm 22:23 (NLT)

It is our responsibility as believers to praise and glorify the majesty of God. Give thanks and praise for redemption through Christ.

What man is he that **feareth the LORD?** him shall he teach in the way that he shall choose.

Psalm 25:12 (KJV)

We worship the majesty of God by surrendering ourselves to His authority, in this way we are open to receive His instruction on the ways we should go.

———————♦———————

The secret of the LORD is for those who **fear Him,** And He will make them know His covenant.

Psalm 25:14 (NASB)

Wisdom and understanding belong to those who receive the truth and worship the Lord.

———————♦———————

How great is the goodness you have stored up for those who **fear you.** You lavish it on those who come to you for protection, blessing them before the watching world.

Psalm 31:19 (NLT)

Treasures are stored up in the coming world for those who trust God and rely on His grace. He protects those in this world who love Him as a testimony to those around them.

Let all the earth **fear the LORD**: let all the inhabitants of the world stand in awe of him.

Psalm 33:8 (KJV)

Worship and glorify Him who created the heavens and the earth.

———————◆———————

Behold, the eye of the LORD is upon them that **fear him**, upon them that hope in his mercy; To deliver their soul from death, and to keep them alive in famine.

Psalm 33:18-19 (KJV)

God watches over those that worship Him and place their hope in His love. He is able to sustain us and keep our souls safe for eternity.

———————◆———————

For the angel of the Lord is a guard; he surrounds and defends all **who fear him**.

Psalm 34:7 (NLT)

In obedience to God the angels of the Lord watch over those who worship Him, they serve and protect against the power of evil.

Taste and see that the Lord is good. Oh, the joys of those who take refuge in him! **Fear the Lord**, you his godly people, for those who **fear him** will have all they need.

Psalm 34:8-9 (NLT)

See and savor the goodness of the Lord! Let Him be your comfort, for He blesses those who worship and trust in Him.

———◆———

Come, you children, listen to me; I will teach you the **fear of the LORD**.

Psalm 34:11 (NKJV)

Just as David taught the children the fear of the Lord, let it be our desire to demonstrate our reverence for Him to others.

———◆———

Sin whispers to the wicked, deep within their hearts. They have no **fear of God** at all. In their blind conceit, they cannot see how wicked they really are.

Psalm 36:1-2 (NLT)

Because they do not fear and worship the Lord, the wicked are blind to their sin. But a day will come when their sin is revealed to them.

And He has put a new song in my mouth, a song of praise to our God. Many shall see and **fear** (revere and worship) and put their trust and confident reliance in **the Lord**.

Psalm 40:3 (AMP)

Make God your hope, worship and trust in Him even during extended hardship. Rejoice knowing that you are secured by the sacrifice of Christ.

———————◆———————

The righteous will see and **fear**; they will laugh at you, saying, "Here now is the one who did not make God his stronghold but trusted in his great wealth and grew strong by destroying others!"

Psalm 52:6-7 (TNIV)

Worship the Lord; depend on Him for safety, not in your own strength or wealth, or in your own wicked ways.

He will bring me safely back from the battles that I fight against so many enemies. God, who has ruled from eternity, will hear me and defeat them; for they refuse to change, and they do not **fear him**.

Psalm 55:18-19 (GNT)

Though attacks are mounted on all fronts, the God of Heaven rescues those who call Him Lord. The enemy is destined for defeat because they will not turn and worship Him.

———————◆———————

You have given a banner to those who **fear You**, That it may be displayed because of the truth.

Psalm 60:4 (NKJV)

Christ is our banner we proudly raise! He is our example of honor, unity and love who provides strength, courage and ultimate victory against evil.

———————◆———————

For You have heard my vows, O God; You have given me the inheritance of those who **fear Your name**.

Psalm 61:5 (NASB)

Through Christ we commit ourselves to the Father with promises of obedience. What better blessing is there than the inheritance that is reserved for those who worship the Lord.

Those living far away **fear your wonders**; where morning dawns and evening fades you call forth songs of joy.

Psalm 65:8 (NIV)

From the ends of the earth we stand in awe at your wondrous signs and miracles. Day in and day out we worship You! You are the daybreak and the sunset of the day that never ends.

————◆————

Come and hear, all you who **fear God**, And I will declare what He has done for my soul.

Psalm 66:16 (NKJV)

The psalmist was given a heart for prayer, worship the Lord and encourage others by declaring the spiritual blessings God has provided to you.

You, even You, **are to be feared** [with awe and reverence]! Who may stand in Your presence when once Your anger is roused? You caused sentence to be heard from heaven; the earth feared and was still-- When God arose to [establish] judgment, to save all the meek and oppressed of the earth. Selah [pause, and calmly think of that]!

Psalm 76:7-9 (AMP)

You alone are to be worshiped; we stand in awe of Your greatness and give thanks for salvation through Christ. Be still, and know that God, is God!

———◆———

Give the Lord your God what you promised him; bring gifts to him, all you nearby nations. God makes everyone **fear him**; he humbles proud princes and terrifies great kings.

Psalm 76:11-12 (GNT)

Honor God and praise His name, give Him your heart and your prayers, for only He is worthy of your worship and devotion.

Surely His salvation is near to those who **fear Him**,
That glory may dwell in our land.

Psalm 85:9 (NKJV)

Glory dwells with those who worship the Lord,
those who have salvation in Christ. He is with us!

———————◆———————

A God **greatly feared** and revered in the council of
the holy (angelic) ones, and **to be feared** and
worshipfully revered above all those who are round
about Him?

Psalm 89:7 (AMP)

Even the angels in heaven fear and worship the
Lord, they praise His mighty name. Let us be filled with
a holy awe and give Him the honor that only He is
worthy of.

———————◆———————

Who considers the power of your anger, and your
wrath according to the **fear of you**?

Psalm 90:11 (ESV)

Your power is so great! We cannot even
comprehend it! Let our worship be an acceptable
offering to You Lord, even though you deserve so much
more.

For the LORD is great, and greatly to be praised: he is **to be feared** above all gods. For all the gods of the nations are idols: but the LORD made the heavens.

Psalm 96:4-5 (KJV)

Praise the Lord, for He is great! No other god can compare to the one God who is the author of all creation. Only He is deserving of our honor and worship.

For as high as the heavens are above the earth, so great is his love for those **who fear him**;

Psalm 103:11 (NIV)

The abundance of God's mercy and love toward those that worship Him is beyond comprehension, it far exceeds anything we are worthy of.

The Lord is like a father to his children, tender and compassionate to those who **fear him**.

Psalm 103:13 (NLT)

Just as a father provides comfort and forgiveness to a child, so the Lord has love and compassion for those that worship Him.

But the mercy of the LORD is from everlasting to everlasting upon them that **fear him**, and his righteousness unto children's children; To such as keep his covenant, and to those that remember his commandments to do them.

Psalm 103:17-18 (KJV)

God grants His mercies on those that fear the Lord, those who are faithful and hold fast to His commands. His mercies extend from this life to the next, and to our children and to their children provided they worship the Lord.

———◆———

He has given food and provision to those who reverently and worshipfully **fear Him**; He will remember His covenant forever and imprint it [on His mind].

Psalm 111:5 (AMP)

God's love and mercies belong to those who worship Him, He knows our needs and His word is our daily bread that refines and enriches us.

The **fear of the LORD** is the beginning of wisdom; all those who practice it have a good understanding. His praise endures forever!

Psalm 111:10 (ESV)

Good sense and sound judgment belong to those who worship the Lord and are mindful of His commandments. Let the love of God reign in your life.

———◆———

Praise the LORD! Blessed is the man who **fears the LORD**, Who delights greatly in His commandments.

Psalm 112:1 (NKJV)

Blessed are those that worship the Lord, who are content to be under God's direction and are most comfortable when serving Him. Blessed are they who stand in awe of His majesty and make His will, theirs.

———◆———

You who **fear the LORD**, trust in the LORD! He is their help and their shield.

Psalm 115:11 (ESV)

Trust in the Lord, He is our help and protector. Let your faith and boldness for God be a testimony to others.

He will bless them that **fear the LORD,** both small and great.

Psalm 115:13 (KJV)

All who honor and worship God receive his blessing, regardless of how young or mature they are in the Lord.

———◆———

You throw away the wicked of the world like trash. So I will love your rules. I shake in **fear of you;** I respect your laws.

Psalm 119:119-120 (NCV)

Worship the Lord, stand in awe before Him. Observe and follow His ways to guide and keep us from sin.

How joyful are those who **fear the Lord**—all who follow his ways! You will enjoy the fruit of your labor. How joyful and prosperous you will be! Your wife will be like a fruitful grapevine, flourishing within your home. Your children will be like vigorous young olive trees as they sit around your table. That is the Lord's blessing for those who **fear him**.

Psalm 128:1-4 (NLT)

Celebrate and cherish the blessings from the Lord, enjoy the fruits of wisdom and goodness. Worship Him and walk in His ways always.

———◆———

Lord, if you kept a record of our sins, who, O Lord, could ever survive? But you offer forgiveness, that we might learn to **fear you**.

Psalm 130:3-4 (NLT)

We worship the Lord and humble ourselves before Him, giving thanks and praise for His mercy and patience, and for redemption through Christ.

He fulfills the desire of those who **fear him**; he also hears their cry and saves them. The LORD preserves all who love him, but all the wicked he will destroy.

Psalm 145:19-20 (ESV)

God is there to hear our prayers, so with all sincerity call out to Him in faith. He preserves and protects those who love and worship Him.

————◆————

The Lord takes pleasure in those who reverently and worshipfully **fear Him**, in those who hope in His mercy and loving-kindness.

Psalm 147:11 (AMP)

The Lord delights in those who worship and place their trust in Him; they place their hope in His mercy and are confident of His goodness.

————◆————

The **fear of the LORD** is the beginning of knowledge: but fools despise wisdom and instruction.

Proverbs 1:7 (KJV)

The wise are those who pursue God and are obedient to His word. They place Him in a high place and approach Him with humility, seeking His perspective rather than acting on their own judgment. God's word is reliable.

Then they will call upon me, but I will not answer; they will seek me diligently but will not find me. Because they hated knowledge and did not choose the **fear of the LORD**, would have none of my counsel and despised all my reproof, therefore they shall eat the fruit of their way, and have their fill of their own devices.

Proverbs 1:28-31 (ESV)

Those who choose to walk in the way of the world lack wisdom, their stubbornness will lead to their downfall. Worship the Lord and walk in His ways.

———◆———

Look for it as hard as you would for silver or some hidden treasure. If you do, you will know what it means to **fear the Lord** and you will succeed in learning about God.

Proverbs 2:4-5 (GNT)

Worship the Lord and seek His will and understanding with enthusiasm and determination.

Don't be impressed with your own wisdom. Instead, **fear the Lord** and turn away from evil. Then you will have healing for your body and strength for your bones.

Proverbs 3:7-8 (NLT)

Do not rely on your own understanding but have confidence in the counsel of God and abandon your evil ways. A virtuous life is good for both a healthy body and a healthy soul.

————◆————

I, wisdom, dwell with prudence, And find out knowledge and discretion. The **fear of the LORD** is to hate evil; Pride and arrogance and the evil way And the perverse mouth I hate.

Proverbs 8:12-13 (NKJV)

Worship the Lord and discover knowledge and discretion. Wisdom hates the evil ways of others, be sure to hate them in yourself.

————◆————

The **fear of the LORD** is the beginning of wisdom: and the knowledge of the holy is understanding.

Proverbs 9:10 (KJV)

We gain understanding when we fill our minds with the word of God and serve Him.

The **fear of the LORD** adds length to life, but the years of the wicked are cut short.

Proverbs 10:27 (TNIV)

The hopes of the wicked turn to disappointment, but the hopes of the righteous are joyful and eternal. Our life on earth is content and gratifying because of the love of the Lord.

————◆————

Whoever walks in uprightness **fears the LORD**, but he who is devious in his ways despises him.

Proverbs 14:2 (ESV)

You will know a person by their walk, where grace reigns there is worship and honor for God, where sin reigns there is contempt for the Lord.

————◆————

The wise **fear the LORD** and shun evil, but a fool is hotheaded and yet feels secure.

Proverbs 14:16 (TNIV)

The wise worship the Lord and run from evil and from the temptation of it, but a fool defies God even when warned.

In the reverent and worshipful **fear of the Lord** there is strong confidence, and His children shall always have a place of refuge.

Proverbs 14:26 (AMP)

Our reverential walk with God provides confidence and peace of mind no matter what happens.

———————◆———————

Reverent and worshipful **fear of the Lord** is a fountain of life, that one may avoid the snares of death.

Proverbs 14:27 (AMP)

When we worship God our souls are showered with joy and everlasting happiness.

———————◆———————

The **fear of the LORD** is the instruction of wisdom; and before honour is humility.

Proverbs 15:33 (KJV)

Worshiping the Lord results in wisdom, a guide to discipline your life; humility brings you honor.

By mercy and love, truth and fidelity [to God and man--not by sacrificial offerings], iniquity is purged out of the heart, and by the reverent, worshipful **fear of the Lord** men depart from and avoid evil.

Proverbs 16:6 (AMP)

The grip of sin is broken through the mercy and truth of Christ's sacrifice, not because of anything we do on our own. Evil departs those who worship the Lord.

The **fear of the LORD** leads to life, and whoever has it rests satisfied; he will not be visited by harm.

Proverbs 19:23 (ESV)

Evil does not reside within those who worship the Lord for we are filled with the love of God that provides satisfaction and eternal life.

The reward for humility and **fear of the LORD** is riches and honor and life.

Proverbs 22:4 (ESV)

We humble ourselves before the greatness of God and receive His riches, comfort and life in this world as much and for as long as He wishes, and look forward to the fulfillment of His promise of eternal life in the next.

Do not let your heart envy sinners, But live in the **fear of the LORD** always. Surely there is a future, And your hope will not be cut off.

Proverbs 23:17-18 (NASB)

Do not envy or adopt the practices of those who sin even though they may prosper in this life, but worship the Lord and do His will and your reward will outshine anything imaginable.

————◆————

My son, [reverently] **fear the Lord** and the king, and do not associate with those who are given to change [of allegiance, and are revolutionary], For their calamity shall rise suddenly, and who knows the punishment and ruin which both [the Lord and the king] will bring upon [the rebellious]?

Proverbs 24:21-22 (AMP)

Beware of any man that promotes a religion of convenience for it only leads to destruction. Honor and worship the God of Heaven who never changes.

Blessed is the one who **fears the LORD** always, but whoever hardens his heart will fall into calamity.

Proverbs 28:14 (ESV)

The Lord blesses those who worship the Lord, they are happy regardless of circumstances.

———————◆———————

Charm is deceitful and beauty is vain, But a woman who **fears the LORD**, she shall be praised.

Proverbs 31:30 (NASB)

Charm can mislead and outward beauty fades away, but when God is worshiped and reigns in your heart you have inner beauty, beauty of the soul.

———————◆———————

I know that everything God does will remain forever; there is nothing to add to it and there is nothing to take from it, for God has so worked that men should **fear Him**.

Ecclesiastes 3:14 (NASB)

Nothing in the world can change anything God desires, our obligation is to submit to His will and worship Him and keep our eyes always on Him. Our God endures forever!

Do not be excessively righteous and do not be overly wise. Why should you ruin yourself? Do not be excessively wicked and do not be a fool. Why should you die before your time? It is good that you grasp one thing and also not let go of the other; for the one who **fears God** comes forth with both of them.

Ecclesiastes 7:16-18 (NASB)

Let wisdom, which comes from having a worshipful heart for God, be your guide when making decisions in order to protect your Christian character and witness.

————————◆————————

But even though a person sins a hundred times and still lives a long time, I know that those who **fear God** will be better off. The wicked will not prosper, for they do not fear God. Their days will never grow long like the evening shadows.

Ecclesiastes 8:12-13 (NLT)

The corrupt of the world will be judged for their evil deeds, their days are numbered. Believers do not fear what the corrupt can do; it will be well with us. We worship God and know that our days will not be cut short for we have the promise of everlasting life.

That's the whole story. Here now is my final conclusion: **Fear God** and obey his commands, for this is everyone's duty. God will judge us for everything we do, including every secret thing, whether good or bad.

Ecclesiastes 12:13-14 (NLT)

Worship the Lord, submit to His majesty, obey His commands for all will be judged, all will be exposed, even our most private thoughts. Walk with Him today and you will have nothing to fear.

—————◆—————

With his great power the LORD warned me not to follow the road which the people were following. He said, "Do not join in the schemes of the people and do not be afraid of the things that they fear. Remember that I, the LORD Almighty, am holy; **I am the one you must fear.**"

Isaiah 8:11-13 (GNT)

The Lord is our Maker, make Him the object of your fear and stand in awe of His supreme power, which overshadows the fear of our enemies.

And the spirit of the LORD shall rest upon him, the spirit of wisdom and understanding, the spirit of counsel and might, the spirit of knowledge and of the **fear of the LORD**; And shall make him of quick understanding in the **fear of the LORD**: and he shall not judge after the sight of his eyes, neither reprove after the hearing of his ears:

Isaiah 11:2-3 (KJV)

All the gifts and grace of the Holy Spirit abide in Christ, our counselor. He is our example of courage and truth in advancing the gospel and our encouragement in worshiping the Lord.

———————◆———————

The LORD is exalted, for he dwells on high; he will fill Zion with justice and righteousness. He will be the sure foundation for your times, a rich store of salvation and wisdom and knowledge; the **fear of the LORD** is the key to this treasure.

Isaiah 33:5-6 (NIV)

The Lord is the foundation on which we stand; He is fair and just, always protecting His people and providing wisdom and knowledge to those who worship Him.

Who among you **fears the LORD**? Who obeys the voice of His Servant? Who walks in darkness And has no light? Let him trust in the name of the LORD And rely upon his God.

Isaiah 50:10 (NKJV)

Child of God, be encouraged! Place your confidence and trust in the name of the Lord and stand in awe of His majesty and grace.

———◆———

"Are you afraid of these idols? Do they terrify you? Is that why you have lied to me and forgotten me and my words? Is it because of my long silence that you no longer **fear me**? Now I will expose your so-called good deeds. None of them will help you. Let's see if your idols can save you when you cry to them for help. Why, a puff of wind can knock them down! If you just breathe on them, they fall over! But whoever trusts in me will inherit the land and possess my holy mountain."

Isaiah 57:11-13 (NLT)

Those who put their faith in idols dishonor God, their lies will be exposed and no one will be able to help them. Those who trust and worship the Lord honor Him and have an inheritance.

From east to west everyone will **fear him** and his great power. He will come like a rushing river, like a strong wind. The Lord says to his people, I will come to Jerusalem to defend you and to save all of you that turn from your sins. And I make a covenant with you: I have given you my power and my teachings to be yours forever, and from now on you are to obey me and teach your children and your descendants to obey me for all time to come.

Isaiah 59:19-21 (GNT)

Empowered by the Spirit we share the gospel message of Christ who was sent on our behalf to defend against evil, so that across the earth all will bow down and worship the Father.

Do you not **fear and reverence Me**? says the Lord. Do you not tremble before Me? I placed the sand for the boundary of the sea, a perpetual barrier beyond which it cannot pass and by an everlasting ordinance beyond which it cannot go? And though the waves of the sea toss and shake themselves, yet they cannot prevail [against the feeble grains of sand which God has ordained by nature to be sufficient for His purpose]; though [the billows] roar, yet they cannot pass over that [barrier]. [Is not such a God to be **reverently feared** and worshiped?]

Jeremiah 5:22 (AMP)

Even the waves know the boundaries that God has established for them; therefore discipline yourself and exercise the fear of God that He has instilled within you. May the greatness of the Lord be worshipped!

"Their gods are like helpless scarecrows in a cucumber field! They cannot speak, and they need to be carried cause they cannot walk. Do not be afraid of such gods, for they can neither harm you nor do you any good." Lord, there is no one like you! For you are great, and your name is full of power. **Who would not fear you**, O King of nations? That title belongs to you alone! Among all the wise people of the earth and in all the kingdoms of the world, there is no one like you.

Jeremiah 10:5-7 (NLT)

Who could think to worship anyone besides the God whose kingdom rules over all things! Our God is the living God and eternal King, be devoted and worship Him alone for there is no one like Him. He has power over all things.

————◆————

Hezekiah king of Judah and the people of Judah did not kill Micah. You know that Hezekiah **feared the Lord** and tried to please the Lord. So the Lord changed his mind and did not bring on Judah the disaster he had promised. If we hurt Jeremiah, we will bring a terrible disaster on ourselves!

Jeremiah 26:19 (NCV)

Worship the Lord and heed the call of His Spirit to avoid sin, consider the consequences and the harm it brings to us and our witness.

And they shall be my people, and I will be their God: And I will give them one heart, and one way, that they may **fear me** for ever, for the good of them, and of their children after them: And I will make an everlasting covenant with them, that I will not turn away from them, to do them good; but I will **put my fear in their hearts**, that they shall not depart from me. Yea, I will rejoice over them to do them good, and I will plant them in this land assuredly with my whole heart and with my whole soul.

Jeremiah 32:38-41 (KJV)

God shapes the hearts of men to worship Him and Him alone. Those who worship Him have His promise of peace and security and to work things for their good.

———————◆———————

I am making a new law for people in every part of my kingdom. All of you must **fear and respect the God of Daniel.** Daniel's God is the living God; he lives forever. His kingdom will never be destroyed, and his rule will never end. God rescues and saves people and does mighty miracles in heaven and on earth. He is the one who saved Daniel from the power of the lions.

Daniel 6:26-27 (NCV)

Worship the Lord and walk according to His ways, trust Him and turn your heart from earthly treasures. He is able to deliver His people from trouble and worry, the sovereign Lord reigns forever!

So they took up Jonah, and cast him forth into the sea: and the sea ceased from her raging. Then the men **feared the LORD** exceedingly, and offered a sacrifice unto the LORD, and made vows.

Jonah 1:15-16 (KJV)

Cast your fear and worry on to God and allow Him to calm the storm in your life. Worship the Lord and give Him thanks for the cross upon which our sins were thrust upon.

————◆————

I said, 'Surely you will **fear me**; you will accept correction. Then your dwelling would not be cut off according to all that I have appointed against you.' But all the more they were eager to make all their deeds corrupt.

Zephaniah 3:7 (ESV)

Heeding a word of correction and turning from sin is evidence of worship for the Lord.

"The person who cheats will be cursed. He has a male animal in his flock and promises to offer it, but then he offers to the Lord an animal that has something wrong with it. I am a great king," says the Lord All-Powerful, "and **I am feared** by all the nations."

Malachi 1:14 (NCV)

God's gifts are priceless, offer Him worship that is reverent and genuine, otherwise you only deceive yourself.

———————◆———————

"At that time I will put you on trial. I am eager to witness against all sorcerers and adulterers and liars. I will speak against those who cheat employees of their wages, who oppress widows and orphans, or who deprive the foreigners living among you of justice, for these people do not **fear me**," says the Lord of Heaven's Armies.

Malachi 3:5 (NLT)

The root of all evil is that men do not worship the Lord; He will be a witness against those that do not fear Him because He knows all things. Reverently worship the Lord and evil will retreat in fear.

Then those who **feared the Lord** spoke with each other, and the Lord listened to what they said. In his presence, a scroll of remembrance was written to record the names of **those who feared him** and always thought about the honor of his name.

Malachi 3:16 (NLT)

When we worship the Lord and keep Him close to our hearts we honor Him and enjoy His fellowship and intimacy.

———————◆———————

And fear not them which kill the body, but are not able to kill the soul: but rather **fear him** which is able to destroy both soul and body in hell.

Matthew 10:28 (KJV)

The fear of man can be a deceptive trap that draws us into sin. Instead, have a sincere faith in Christ and never be ashamed of your relationship with Him, for those who truly worship God need not fear any man.

Jesus got up and ordered the wind and the waves to be quiet. The wind stopped, and everything was calm. Jesus asked his disciples, "Why were you afraid? Don't you have any faith?" Now they were **more afraid than ever** and said to each other, "Who is this? Even the wind and the waves obey him!"

Mark 4:39-41 (CEV)

When we have faith in ALL matters our fears turn to calm. Stand in awe and give honor and praise to God who is gracious and all powerful.

———◆———

For He Who is almighty has done great things for me--and holy is His name [to be venerated in His purity, majesty and glory]! And His mercy (His compassion and kindness toward the miserable and afflicted) is on those who **fear Him** with godly reverence, from generation to generation and age to age.

Luke 1:49-50 (AMP)

The idea that God would use us to achieve His will fills us with wonder. His mercy, through Christ, for all generations is worthy of our praise and worship.

And they came to Him and awoke Him, saying, "Master, Master, we are perishing!" Then He arose and rebuked the wind and the raging of the water. And they ceased, and there was a calm. But He said to them, "Where is your faith?" And **they were afraid, and marveled**, saying to one another, "Who can this be? For He commands even the winds and water, and they obey Him!"

Luke 8:24-25 (NKJV)

Put your faith in Christ and give Him the glory, for He is able to calm the storms of fear. Watch and be amazed at His power!

———————◆———————

I tell you, my friends, do not be afraid of those who kill the body and after that can do no more. But I will show you whom you should fear: **Fear him** who, after the killing of the body, has power to throw you into hell. Yes, I tell you, **fear him**.

Luke 12:4-5 (NIV)

We have a friend in Jesus, so be bold in your faith walk and worship the One who is all powerful and in control, those who have a holy fear of God need not fear any man.

But the other criminal protested, "Don't you **fear God** even when you have been sentenced to die? We deserve to die for our crimes, but this man hasn't done anything wrong." Then he said, "Jesus, remember me when you come into your Kingdom." And Jesus replied, "I assure you, today you will be with me in paradise."

Luke 23:40-43 (NLT)

In this life there is still hope, still time to repent, time to pray and to find faith in Christ who died for us. Our hope is in Him and to the next life.

———◆———

After forty years had passed, an angel appeared to Moses in the flames of a burning bush in the desert near Mount Sinai. When he saw this, he was amazed at the sight. As he went over to look more closely, he heard the Lord's voice: "I am the God of your fathers, the God of Abraham, Isaac and Jacob." Moses **trembled with fear** and did not dare to look.

Acts 7:30-32 (NIV)

God is the same yesterday and today, listen to His spirit and be refined through faith. Exalt the majesty and glory of God!

The church then had peace throughout Judea, Galilee, and Samaria, and it became stronger as the believers lived in the **fear of the Lord**. And with the encouragement of the Holy Spirit, it also grew in numbers.

Acts 9:31 (NLT)

A faithful walk with God provides the comfort and confidence of His Spirit. Our faith and the entire church are built up when we worship the Lord.

———————◆———————

Opening his mouth, Peter said: "I most certainly understand now that God is not one to show partiality, but in every nation the man who **fears Him** and does what is right is welcome to Him.

Acts 10:34-35 (NASB)

God has no favorites, He welcomes all who worship Him and are faithful.

There is no **fear of God** before their eyes.

Romans 3:18 (KJV)

When we worship the Lord our lives are governed and directed by His will and for His glory. We see that we are all sinners made right not by anything we can do, but only through Christ.

———————◆———————

You will say then, Branches were broken (pruned) off so that I might be grafted in! That is true. But they were broken (pruned) off because of their unbelief (their lack of real faith), and you are established through faith [because you do believe]. So do not become proud and conceited, but rather **stand in awe and be reverently afraid**. For if God did not spare the natural branches [because of unbelief], neither will He spare you [if you are guilty of the same offense].

Romans 11:19-21 (AMP)

We are not saved by anything we have done, only because of our belief and because of God's grace are we grafted into His covenant. Do not count on your own strength but give thanks and worship the Lord always for fear of being cut off as unbelievers are.

For the authorities do not strike fear in people who are doing right, but in those who are doing wrong. Would you like to live without fear of the authorities? Do what is right, and they will honor you. The authorities are God's servants, sent for your good. But if you are doing wrong, of course you should be afraid, for they have the power to punish you. They are God's servants, sent for the very purpose of punishing those who do what is wrong. So you must **submit** to them, not only to avoid punishment, but **also to keep a clear conscience**.

Romans 13:3-5 (NLT)

God places those he wants in positions of government to accomplish His greater purpose. Only those that do wrong need to fear punishment. In the same way we are subject to following God's authority established for His kingdom, so through obedience, we worship Him.

I want you to be free from anxieties. The unmarried man is **anxious about the things of the Lord**, how to please the Lord. But the married man is anxious about worldly things, how to please his wife, and his interests are divided. And the unmarried or betrothed woman is **anxious about the things of the Lord**, how to be holy in body and spirit. But the married woman is anxious about worldly things, how to please her husband. I say this for your own benefit, not to lay any restraint upon you, but to promote good order **and to secure your undivided devotion to the Lord**.

1 Corinthians 7:32-35 (ESV)

Seek wisdom regarding your earthly responsibilities, be careful not to worry or be overly consumed with things of the world. Fewer interests in the world will allow you to place more of your attention on pleasing and worshiping God.

For we must all appear before the judgment seat of Christ, so that each one may receive what is due for what he has done in the body, whether good or evil. Therefore, knowing the **fear of the Lord**, we persuade others. But what we are is known to God, and I hope it is known also to your conscience.

2 Corinthians 5:10-11 (ESV)

You know that one day everyone will stand in judgment, so in worship to God be an encouragement to others so that they will be ready to face God.

———————◆———————

Slaves, obey your earthly masters **with respect and fear**, and with sincerity of heart, just as you would **obey Christ**.

Ephesians 6:5 (TNIV)

Be sincere and cheerful in your work. Remember that regardless of who you are working for, you are really working for the Lord. Serve Him with all respect and ability, for a reward awaits you.

Dear friends, you always followed my instructions when I was with you. And now that I am away, it is even more important. Work hard to show the results of your salvation, obeying God **with deep reverence and fear**. For God is working in you, giving you the desire and the power to do what pleases him.

Philippians 2:12-13 (NLT)

We worship Him when, through God's grace, we willingly demonstrate our salvation by being careful and vigilant in performing His work.

———————◆———————

Who in the days of his flesh, when he had offered up prayers and supplications with strong crying and tears unto him that was able to save him from death, and was heard in that **he feared**; Though he were a Son, yet learned he obedience by the things which he suffered;

Hebrews 5:7-8 (KJV)

God hears the prayers of those that worship Him. The intensity of Christ's prayers brought comfort from God so that He could be obedient to suffering and saved from death.

Therefore, since we are receiving a kingdom which cannot be shaken, let us have grace, by which we may serve God acceptably with **reverence and godly fear**.

Hebrews 12:28 (NKJV)

Only by the grace of God are we made right with Him. For that reason, we worship Him with holy fear and godly reverence.

————◆————

Since you call on a Father who judges each man's work impartially, live your lives as strangers here in **reverent fear**.

1 Peter 1:17 (NIV)

Like workers in a foreign land, our mission and obligation is to serve the Lord through faith and obedience during our short time here.

————◆————

Honour all men. Love the brotherhood. **Fear God**. Honour the king.

1 Peter 2:17 (KJV)

Be of good character and live your life with integrity, treating everyone the same, with dignity. Love your brothers and sisters in Christ and be respectful of authority. Honor and revere the Lord God!

Saying with a loud voice, **Fear God**, and give glory to him; for the hour of his judgment is come: and worship him that made heaven, and earth, and the sea, and the fountains of waters.

Revelation 14:7 (KJV)

We look forward to the day when ALL will worship and give glory and honor to Him, offering praise to He who made heaven, earth and sea.

———◆———

Who will not **fear you**, O Lord, and bring glory to your name? For you alone are holy. All nations will come and worship before you, for your righteous acts have been revealed.

Revelation 15:4 (NIV)

Stand in awe of the Lord and declare His name great, for He alone is holy and worthy of worship by all peoples.

———◆———

And from the throne came a voice saying, "Praise our God, all you his servants, you who **fear him**, small and great."

Revelation 19:5 (ESV)

Worship and honor Him who is worthy! He is triumphant and deserving of praise!

Scripture Versions

Index

215

www.fearfultofearless.com